GROWING

*A comprehensive
parish youth programme*

SUSAN SAYERS

Drawings by Arthur Baker

First published in Great Britain in 1992 by
KEVIN MAYHEW LTD
Rattlesden, Bury St Edmunds,
Suffolk IP30 0SZ

ISBN 0 86209 156 X

The scripture texts in this
book are the author's own translations.

Cover design by Graham Johnstone
Typesetting by Typestylers, Ipswich, and Anne Haskell
Printed and bound in Hong Kong by Colorcraft.

CONTENTS

Introduction

PART ONE: LEADERS' NOTES

Units

PART TWO: RESOURCE SHEETS

Units

PART THREE: FRANCIS!

INTRODUCTION

Sadly, children and young people are often talked of as the Church of the future. One might just as well talk of senior citizens as those who used to be the Church when they were younger! We need to delight in the fact that the living stones of our Church include not only rocks and boulders, but pebbles as well; children and young people are undoubtedly essential and valuable members of the Church of the present.

Perhaps due to this misconception, programmes for young people are often based on the assumption that the adult leaders are those 'in the know' and their task is to pass on the teaching and heritage of the Church. The danger here is that we get a one-way system of learning. Yet several times in the gospels Jesus emphasises our need to become like children if we are to enter the kingdom. Could it be that we are losing out on what our children and young people can teach us?

Obviously we all need to build one another up in the faith, and age should be no more a barrier in this than sex, race or intelligence. We need to create a climate where faith can develop to maturity, not just in the young but also in the elderly. And often it is the directness and enthusiasm of the young which can rekindle faltering faith, insist on integrity, and draw attention to any flourishing weeds which threaten to choke the growth of good grain.

This material is designed to be a resource for young people and to encourage their ministry as full, active members of the Church.

WHAT IS IN THIS BOOK?

PART 1 LEADERS' NOTES
The material is arranged in eight units, each on a different theme. Each unit includes ideas for activities, discussion, worship and games, and each works towards producing some kind of resource for the parish or school. In the leaders' notes there are clear instructions and practical hints for organising each topic.

PART 2 RESOURCE SHEETS
These sheets are copyright-free, so that you can duplicate as many as you need for the group, providing they are only used locally for school or parish work. (Reproduction of these sheets for commercial purposes is subject to the usual copyright regulations.) The sheets provide the basis for the 'Thinking Things Out' discussions, and also for the worship, and there are six sheets to accompany each unit.

PART 3 FRANCIS!
This is the musical play which forms the core of Unit 5. The full text and music is given, followed by performing notes and dance sequences. Permission to copy or reproduce all or part of this section must be sought from the publishers in advance.

HOW DO I USE THE MATERIAL?

The material is designed to be as flexible as possible. Since each topic unit is completely self-contained, there are many different ways of using them. For example:

● A particular unit, with six sessions of intensive activity, can be slotted into an existing youth programme; perhaps during Lent, as a preparation or follow-up confirmation course, or as part of a parish mission programme.
● Particular units can be used as GCSE course work resource material, or as part of a more general RE syllabus.
● Alternatively, the units can be taken at a slower pace, and become a regular feature of a church youth club, with each unit covering 12 sessions.
● On a week-long retreat or holiday club for young people, one unit would provide a complete programme for six days' activity.
● Where there is as yet little going on for young people, or where leaders lack confidence, or where people are hesitant about long-term commitments, one unit can be a 'taster' course which may well grow into a more regular group.
● Although all components of a unit are designed to complement one another, it is of course possible to use the activities, the games, or the 'Thinking Things Out' and worship sessions on their own, according to your needs.

I'M NEW TO THIS — WHERE DO I START?

With prayer! Unless we are attentive to God's ways and God's timing, we can easily find ourselves rushing about our own business instead of doing his. Working with him is altogether easier and more enjoyable. Thinking and planning prayerfully will highlight the real needs of the parish, the young people who need to be contacted, and those who will be the leaders. It is better to have a few committed leaders than an army of only moderately interested helpers.

Once the team is established, meet to work out what the aim of the group is, both in the short term and in the long term. It is a good idea to put all this in writing so that as the weeks go by you can assess how things are going. After all, experience is a great teacher, as are mistakes.

Take time to choose and plan a complete unit broadly at a leaders' meeting, arranging who will take charge of what, who will contact whom etc. You will then find that each session of the unit runs smoothly without a great workload for anyone. The material is planned to give the leaders freedom to enjoy the activities along with the group.

At first you will probably want to follow the course exactly as it stands. This will give you a good, firm, structure in which to gain confidence in group leadership. Eventually you may wish to use the ideas as starters, developing them yourself.

The discussion questions have been carefully designed to get people talking freely, and every question leads on to the next, so it is best to work through them in order. The leader's role in discussion is that of enabler, not teacher, and it is vital that everything offered in discussion is accepted with respect and treated seriously, even if it is unexpected or unconventional. Some of the questions are deliberately challenging, for growth in faith demands this. Humour and sensitivity are important here, but expect passionate feelings to show. We are, after all, dealing with very powerful matters, and it is essential that young people feel able to discuss their doubts and fears as well as their hopes and convictions.

Pray daily for all those involved with the group, and enjoy the company of each one; it is through being valued, respected and loved that we all learn to value, respect and love others.

MUSIC

Suggestions for hymns, songs and choruses have been made from the following sources:

Alleluya!
HLS (His Light Shines)
HOAN (Hymns Old & New)
MSOTS (More Songs of the Spirit)
MWTP (Many Ways To Praise)
PP (Children's Praise Party)
PP2 (Children's Praise Party Vol 2)
SOF (Songs of Fellowship)
SOF4 (Songs of Fellowship Vol 4)
SOTS (Songs of the Spirit)
SOTS3 (Songs of the Spirit Vol 3)

PART ONE: LEADERS' NOTES

NEWS

AIM

1 To explore the Bible in terms of story telling, history, prophecy and the spreading of the good news of the gospels.

2 To relate this to our own news coverage, and the value of communication.

LENGTH OF UNIT

Six to twelve sessions.

WHAT WILL WE BE DOING?

Making newspapers set at the time of particular events in the Bible. These would be a useful resource as a discussion starter for Bible study groups in the parish.

ACTIVITIES

NEWSPAPER PLANNING

Each newspaper to be produced will need a production team of 4-6 people. Fewer than this makes for too heavy a workload, more gets unmanageable. So the number of newspapers you produce obviously depends on the size of your group. Working to a deadline creates a more exciting, though more stressful atmosphere! Suggested central events:

☐ Escape from Egypt (Exodus 2-15; Psalm 105:26-45).

☐ David's coronation (1 Samuel 16-17; 2 Samuel 1-6).

☐ The fall of Jerusalem and exile to Babylonia (2 Kings 25:2 Chronicles 36; Jeremiah 52; Lamentations 1-5; Psalm 134).

☐ Return from exile and rebuilding the walls (Ezra 1-3; Nehemiah 1-4; Psalms 100, 106, 107, 118, 136).

☐ Bethlehem at Jesus' birth (Matthew, Luke).

☐ Galilee during Jesus' ministry (Matthew, Mark, Luke, John).

☐ Jerusalem at the time of the resurrection (Matthew, Mark, Luke, John).

☐ Early Church (Acts).

I have given Bible references, but you will also find it useful to have a number of history books, pictorial Bible commentaries etc.

Recommended titles:

Look into the Bible (A Young Person's Guide), edited by Eric Gower. Scripture Union, 1988.

Jesus and His Times, edited by Kaari Ward. The Readers Digest Assn Inc., 1989.

Focus on the Bible, by H. J. Richards. Kevin Mayhew, 1989.

The Living World of the Old Testament, by Bernhard W. Anderson. Longman, 1975.

Introducing the New Testament, by John Drane. Lion, 1986.

History of Everyday Life, by Piero Ventura. Kingfisher Books, 1987.

Peoples of the Past (Egyptians, Romans) Macdonald Educational.

Each group needs to collect main stories, interviews, artwork, advertisements, puzzles, editorial articles, social gossip, sport etc so that the newspaper gives a vivid atmosphere of life at the time.

They will need to make sure they are quite well informed before they start, so as to avoid errors that are costly in time and effort. Each group appoints an editor who works on material with the others, and also organises and brings everything together. Depending on the age of the group, it may be useful to have an older assistant for this task, as it demands organisation and leadership without bossiness.

CALLIGRAPHY

If you have access to a computer, word processor or typewriter, this is naturally extremely useful, but hand-written newspapers also look most attractive, especially if they are written with calligraphy pens in a specially chosen script. Calligraphy kits come with a variety of nib thicknesses, and there are some excellent sets of felt tip calligraphy pens with one end for thick and the other for finer work. Scribes need a perfect script to work from, of course, so all secretarial editing should be completed before the scribes begin the final work of art!

NEWSPAPER ARTICLES

Have a look at some newspapers to see the usual format and style. The children's newspapers, *Early Times* and *Indy* are clear and of a high quality.

☐ Look at the central events and pick out the different characters and groups involved. An article from each different viewpoint allows the story to live very convincingly.

☐ Look at the articles people are using in the Bible story; this will give you some ideas for advertisements for jobs, items for sale etc.

☐ Look at the area where the events are taking place; this will give you ideas for a weather forecast, traffic report, business report or flood warning, perhaps.

☐ Look at related past events; whenever a story is covered in the news, facts (or suspicions) are included from the past so as to shed light on present issues.

☐ Look for differences of opinion; imagine an interview with someone from each side, or stage a news conference where the two representatives are allowed to argue their case.

☐ Look for the visual, and draw 'photographs' which catch the mood of the moment.

NEWSPAPER FORMAT

Two sheets of A3 paper make a good sized, 8 page newspaper, though you may decide to make yours bigger. If you want it smaller, it's better to cut down on the number of pages rather than the page size, as anything smaller loses the feel of being a real newspaper.

Work out the width of columns needed and cut paper for articles to size before the scribes or typists begin. Allow plenty of space for headlines, titles, pictures etc.

SEEING THE REAL THING

As part of the unit it would be interesting to visit a publisher, printer or newspaper house, so as to see the professionals in action. You may be able to pick up a few hints. Eventually the firm might like to see the finished newspapers you have made.

SESSION ONE

Have you heard...?

THINKING THINGS OUT

Either play Chinese whispers, where a message is passed by whisper round the whole group and often gets drastically changed in the process; or do the same thing in mime, where 10 people come in one after the other to observe a mime. Each performs what he thinks he has seen to the next person who comes in. Again, the distorting effect is very entertaining.

1 What happened to the message as it was handed on through the group?

2 How does the same kind of thing happen with rumours?

3 If you wanted to make sure a message would be passed down exactly, how would you do it?

To read together: Genesis 27:1-29

4 A family story like this would be handed down carefully, told round fires in the winter evenings, perhaps. Have you been told stories about your great aunt Nelly, or your parents when they were little, which everyone in the family enjoys laughing over? You might like to share them with the person sitting next to you.

5 Which do you enjoy most — news articles about events or people?

6 If you read a false rumour about yourself in a newspaper, how would you feel and what would you do?

7 If we didn't have a written language, why do you think we might value old people as especially important in our community?

8 During the week, ask an elderly relative or friend what s/he can remember about schools, heating, children's jobs, food, homes, games etc. when s/he was a child.

WORSHIP

If possible, gather for worship round a camp fire. If this isn't practical, have an old family photograph album and a lamp or candle in the centre of the circle. Sing together *Joshua fought the battle of Jericho* (Alleluya!) and *Rise and shine* (Alleluya!), so that you are keeping the tradition of enjoying the old family stories of the Bible. After the singing have a time of silence.

Reader 1 Exodus 12:23-27a.

The Lord will pass through the country killing the Egyptians, and when he sees the blood on your doorframes, he will pass over and refuse to let the Destroyer come into your houses to harm you. Both you and your descendants must obey these rules for ever.

Reader 2 And when you arrive at the land which God will give you, just as he has promised, you must keep this ritual. When your children ask you,

Half 'What does this ritual mean?'

Reader 2 you will reply,

Other half 'It is the Passover sacrifice in honour of the Lord, who passed over the houses of the Israelites in Egypt, killing the Egyptians but sparing us.'

Sing together a song or chorus such as:
By the waters of Babylon (HOAN)
Moses I know you're the man (HOAN)
What have they done to the rain? (Alleluya!)
When the Spirit of the Lord (SOF)

Reader 1 Father, we pray for all who work for newspapers, or in broadcasting.

Silence

All Help them to give information with honesty and sensitivity. Open our hearts so that we are responsive to the needs of our world.

SESSION TWO

Heroes and idols

THINKING THINGS OUT

In small groups of three or four, complete the chart on the resource sheet about the heroes of today in Music, Sport, Goodness, Power, and Badness.

1 Who are our society's heroes? Share with one another the different heroes mentioned, writing them all up on a wall chart.

2 Why do we like having heroes and anti-heroes?

3 We sometimes talk of hero 'worship'. How is this similar to/different from worship of God?

4 What is the difference between a hero and an idol?
To read together: Judges 16:1-22.

5 You can imagine what the newspapers would make of Samson! What headlines and sub-headlines might there be if Delilah sold her story to the press?

6 In what ways would Samson appeal to the public?

7 Do you think he was using his gift of strength in the best way?

8 Does our society tempt us to use our gifts to become rich, rather than for a more valuable goal?

9 Can you think of any times when people have decided to use their talents for a good cause? Share these with the group.

WORSHIP

Gather either round the campfire, or round an arrangement of trophies, pop festival programmes, signed photographs etc. grouped at the foot of a large crucifix. Sing together *Thine be the glory* (HOAN) and let the singing fade into a time of silence.

Reader 1 1 Kings 3:23-28.
King Solomon said thoughtfully,

Reader 2 'One of you women says, "This living son is mine — yours is dead", while the other woman claims, "No, that's not true — your son is the dead one — mine is alive!" '

Reader 1 The king asked for a sword. When they brought it to him he declared,

Reader 2 'Split the living child in two, and give half to one woman and half to the other.'

Reader 1 At that the real mother cried out to the king, deeply distressed at the thought of her son coming to harm.

Reader 3 'O my lord king, I would rather you gave the child to the other woman than kill it!'

Reader 1 But the other woman said,

Reader 4 'No, let neither of us have it. Cut it in half.'

Reader 1 Then King Solomon gave his decision.
▽

Reader 2 'Don't kill the child, but give him to the first woman; she must be his real mother.'

Reader 1 All Israel heard about the way the king had dealt with the problem, and they had great respect for him. They could see that he possessed God's wisdom, which enabled him to settle disputes fairly.

Sing together a song or chorus such as:
When the Spirit of the Lord (SOF)
All that I am (HOAN)
Lord I ask, please give me your wisdom (PP 2)
Take my hands (HOAN)

Reader 1 Father, we pray for all famous people and well-known stars.

Silence

All May they not be spoilt and damaged by their fame. Help us to remember that all we have comes from you. We offer ourselves and our talents and skills and weaknesses for you to use for the good of your world. Amen.

SESSION THREE
Gloom, doom, hope and glory

THINKING THINGS OUT

In small groups of three or four, solve the prophet wordsearch, using a Bible to find which words to look for.

1 Who are the prophets in the Bible? Write all the names found on a wallchart, each on an outline of a scroll.

2 What do you think a prophet does? This may be different from what you would expect, so these references will help you: Isaiah 6:8; Isaiah 7:10; Ezekiel 3:22; Hosea 1:2.

3 Why do you think the prophets were not usually popular? Are such people popular today? To read together: Jonah 1.

4 How did Jonah react to being called by God?

5 If you don't want to do something you know you ought to do, are you ever tempted to go as far as possible in the opposite direction?

6 How did God use Jonah as his messenger even while he was running away? (That can also happen to us; God uses us in all kinds of ways.)

7 Dare we speak out for what is right? Even if it means standing alone? Even if it brings insults and persecution?

8 False prophets say only what people want to hear. When does that happen in our society?

9 How can we be sure it really is God who is calling us? Look at these references to help you: Matthew 12:33-35; Matthew 7:15-20.

WORSHIP

Either gather round the fire, or round an arrangement of books and advertisements proclaiming dramatic promises, with one tall candle burning in the centre of them. Sing together Tell out my soul (HOAN) and let the singing fade into silence.

Reader 1 Jeremiah 20:8-9 (Jeremiah complains to the Lord).
Whenever I speak I have to moan and cry out,

Reader 2 'Destruction! Ruin!'

Reader 1 The word of the Lord which I proclaim, makes me ridiculed and insulted every day. So I think to myself,

Reader 2 'I will ignore the Lord and refuse to speak any more in his name.'

Reader 1 But if I do this, his word burns like a fire deep inside my bones, until I am exhausted from holding it in, and can no longer stop myself from speaking out.

Sing together a song or chorus such as:
Be bold, be strong (SOF 4)
Therefore the redeemed (SOF, SOTS)
They shall go out with joy (SOF)
All over the world (HOAN)

Reader 3 Matthew 7:21.

Not all those who say to me, 'Lord, Lord,' will enter into the kingdom of heaven, but only the person who does the will of my Father in heaven.

All Father, when you speak to us,
help us to listen;
when you call us,
give us courage to follow;
speak through our thoughts,
our words and our actions,
so that we do your will. Amen.

SESSION FOUR

Rediscovered treasure

THINKING THINGS OUT

In twos and threes, tell one another about childhood memories of a) when you have lost something very important or precious, and b) of when, through clearing up your bedroom, you have found something you had lost for ages.

1 In the large group, share one or two of the stories if you wish. How did you feel when you realised you had lost something important? How did your body react?

2 Suppose you had just found, buried in your bedroom, something you were supposed to have dealt with ages ago. How might you feel, and what might you do? Write all the suggestions on a wallchart. (They will all probably belong to these three categories:

a) Put it back and forget it.
b) Destroy the evidence.
c) Put things right.

so group them accordingly as they are written.)

To read together: 2 Chronicles 34:1-2; 8; 14-21.

3 It took the very young king, Josiah, to start cleaning the country up. What did his workmen find buried in a corner of the temple storeroom?

4 How did Josiah react to the discovery? (Link this to what you decided in question 2.)

5 Imagine you are King Josiah. How would you go about putting things right, now that the book of Moses, containing God's Law, has been found? To read together: 2 Chronicles 34:22; 29-33.

6 Compare your ideas with the way Josiah himself tackled the problem.

7 Recently we have discovered the vital importance to our survival of rainforests. Having discovered the truth, and realised the harm we are doing, how should we act?

8 How do we feel, and what should we do, when we realise we have not been living as Jesus told us to?

WORSHIP

Either gather round the camp fire, or round an arangement of typical junk — an odd shoe, a couple of tapes, a towel, several books etc. Have a Bible lying on the top. Sing together *The King of love my shepherd is* (HOAN) and let the singing fade into a time of silence.

Reader 1 Luke 15: 11-20 (the lost son, paraphrased).

There was once a man who had two sons. The younger one said to him,

Reader 2 'Father, give me my share of the property now.'

Reader 1 So the man divided his property between his two sons . . . The second son spent everything he had. Then a severe famine spread over that country, and he was left without a thing. So he went to work looking after pigs. He wished he could fill himself with the bean pods the pigs ate, but no one gave him anything to eat. At last he came to his senses and said,

Reader 2 'All my father's hired workers have more than they can eat, and here am I about to starve! I will get up and go to my father and say, ''Father, I have sinned against God and against you. I am no longer fit to be called your son; treat me as one of your hired workers''.'

Reader 1 So he got up and started back to his father.

Sing together a song or chorus such as:
Father God I wonder (SOF)
Spirit of the living God (HOAN)
Lord, I ask, please give me your wisdom (PP Vol. 2)
Lord, when I turn my back on you (HOAN)

Reader 3 Father, we pray for all who have wandered away from you; for all who feel they have travelled too far to be forgiven.

Silence

All Give us all deep sorrow for our sin, and the reassurance of your forgiveness. Amen.

▽

SESSION FIVE
It's Gospel!

THINKING THINGS OUT

First the whole group acts out the healing of the woman in the crowd on the way to Jairus' house. Beforehand choose someone to be the woman who is healed, and explain her role to her, but don't let anyone else know who it is. (Swear her to secrecy, too.) Decide who are going to be Jesus and Peter, and show them what to say, so that they can say it in their own words.

Read the story as everyone is milling around in a narrow area designated a street for the occasion. When the woman touches Jesus' clothes, let the action turn into a role-play, rather than a narration. Reference: Luke 8:42b-48.

1 Ask the different characters how they felt and what went through their minds when Jesus asked who had touched him. (Include Jesus.)

2 If you were in the crowd, how did you feel about the woman? How did your feelings change when Jesus told her to go in peace, because her faith had made her well?

3 Why do you think the woman touched Jesus when he was in a milling crowd?

4 Why did that touch feel different to Jesus from the usual pushing of the crowd? (You could ask whoever played Jesus about this.)
To read together: John 9 (Have different people reading different parts, and everyone reading the 'people' parts.)

5 What kind of person does Jesus appear to be, from our knowledge of him in the gospels? Write up a kind of identikit character on a wallchart, using everyone's ideas. Try to use actual evidence, rather than vague generalisations. It is a good idea to have Bibles handy to look up half-remembered things.

6 Why did many of the Pharisees find it so difficult to believe that Jesus was the Son of God?

7 Why did he attract such a huge following of people, do you think?

WORSHIP

Either gather round the camp fire, or round a Christmas crib, with candles burning near it. Sing together *Father, we love you* (HOAN) and let the singing fade into a time of silence.

Reader 1 John 9:35-38.
Jesus heard that the man had been thrown out, and when he had found him he asked him,

Reader 2 'Do you believe in the Son of God?'

Reader 1 The man answered,

Reader 3 'Who is he, sir? Tell me, so that I may believe in him.'

Reader 1 Jesus said to him,

Reader 2 'You have seen him already. He is the one talking with you now.'

Reader 3 'Lord, I do believe!'

Reader 1 said the man, and he flung himself down before Jesus.

> Sing a song or chorus such as:
> *A man called Jesus* (Garth Hewitt, *Mud on your eyes*)
> *Jubilate Deo* (HOAN)
> *Hosanna, hosanna* (SOF 4)
> *Who is this man?* (MWTP)
> *Lord, the light of your love* (SOF 4)

Reader 1 Lord, open our eyes to see you clearly;

All open our hearts to trust you more.

Reader 1 Lord, open our ears to hear you speaking;

All open our minds to understand.

Reader 1 Lord, you walked as a person among us;

All walk with us every step of our way. Amen.

SESSION SIX
Good news! Good news!

THINKING THINGS OUT

Give each small group a newspaper or magazine article with pictures, which is full of assumptions, prejudices, hints etc. Ask the groups to fill in the chart about it on the resource sheet.

1 In the large group, discuss your findings. How do the articles give a false or destructive message?

2 Why do you think the writer chose to put this slant on the facts?

3 Should Christians refuse to take part in such things as propaganda, advertising or the 'gutter' press? Give your reasons.

To read together: Acts 4:8-20.

4 What is the good news that Peter and John are so excited about? (Look at verse 12 again if you need to.)

5 How have they shown their message in action, as well as in words?

6 Why are the members of the Council so surprised at Peter and John's speech?

7 What had Jesus promised his followers about speaking up for the truth? (Mark 13:11).

8 How do we sometimes give a confused message about God's saving love for the world?

9 Having seen the kind of person Jesus was in the gospels, how do you think Jesus wants you to follow him today?

WORSHIP

Either gather round the camp fire or round an arrangement of newspapers with a Good News Bible among them. Sing together *God's Spirit is in my heart* (HOAN) and let the singing fade into a time of silence.

Reader 1 Acts 16:25-32.

At midnight, Paul and Silas, who were praying, sang a hymn to God, and the other prisoners listened to them. Suddenly there was a violent earth tremor, enough to shake the foundations of the prison. All the doors were flung open and all the prisoners' fetters snapped.

Reader 2 The gaoler, jerked out of sleep, saw all the open prison doors and drew his sword to kill himself, because he thought all the prisoners must have escaped. But Paul shouted out at the top of his voice,

Reader 3 'You mustn't do yourself any harm! We are all here!'

Reader 1 The gaoler asked for some lights, and then rushed in, where he fell at the feet of Paul and Silas, trembling with terror. Then he led them out and said to them,

Reader 4 'Sirs, what do I have to do to be saved?'

Reader 1 They replied,

Reader 3 'Believe in the Lord Jesus, the Christ, and both you and all your family will be saved.'

Reader 1 And they explained the word of the Lord to him and to everyone in his house.

Sing together a song or chorus such as:
O Lord, all the world belongs to you (HOAN)
Take me, Lord, use my life (HOAN)
Go in peace to be Christ's body (HOAN)
Alleluia, Alleluia, give thanks to the risen Lord (HOAN)

Reader 2 Father, we praise you with all our being.

All Use us to spread the good news of your love! Amen.

GAMES

FLAPPING RACE

Cut out of newspaper some shapes of frogs, fish or anything else you wish to race, and fold other newspapers to make effective flappers. Teams have to flap their frog/fish/alien up to the other end of the room one at a time, running back with the flapper ready for the next team member's flap. The winning team is the one to get all their frogs/fish/aliens flapped up to the end of the room first. And no touching!

ORDER!

Have one large Sunday newspaper for each team, and muddle the pages up completely. The aim is to get the paper in order again before anyone else. Teams should be of four or five people.

▽

WHAT D'YER SAY?

Partners sit at opposite sides of the room, in two lines as far away from each other as possible. Give out different written messages to everyone on one side of the room. At the word 'Go' they all look at their messages and shout them across to their partners, who let you know the message as soon as they have understood it. Since everyone is shouting at once, this is not as easy as it seems.

GIVE US A CLUE

Mime the title of a book, programme, film, animal, occupation etc. to the group until someone guesses what your mime represents. Whoever guesses correctly has the next go at miming.

COSTUMES

Give each group plenty of newspaper, sellotape and scissors. Give out a category, such as animal, occupation, historical character etc. They have to dress one member of the group up accordingly, using only the materials provided and in only 15 minutes. Have a fashion parade at the end and choose a winner if you wish.

BRIDGES

Again, provide each group with plenty of newspaper and then give them the challenge of constructing a bridge with a span of at least one metre. The winner is the group that can make the strongest bridge.

NEWSROUND

On the wall, stick up newspaper pictures of well-known news items, and number them. Stick their matching stories around on another wall, and letter them. See how many stories and pictures people can match up.

UNIT TWO

JOURNEYS

AIM

To explore some of the aspects of physical journeys and relate them to our spiritual journey through life.

LENGTH OF UNIT

Six to twelve sessions (plus Pilgrimage).

WHAT WILL WE BE DOING?

We will be planning and preparing for a pilgrimage, which all the parish will be invited to join.

INTRODUCTORY ACTIVITY

Deciding or informing where and when the pilgrimage will be.

1. What IS a pilgrimage, anyway?

Note down all main ideas on a sheet of paper that everyone can see. Having several different dictionaries and encyclopedias available will enable the group to arrive at quite a comprehensive idea of what is usually involved.

2. Where shall we be going?

Slides or photographs, information, brochures etc are important in getting everyone's imagination going. If you are giving the group a choice of destinations it is probably better to limit them to a few practical choices.

> In making your selection of a suitable destination, bear in mind the mixed age group, the spiritual needs of the group and, obviously, such practical matters as cost, proximity and the amount of time available for the pilgrimage.
>
> Don't necessarily go for the obvious choices; there are a great many suitable places of pilgrimage which are seldom or never used in this way.

Here are a few guidelines to start you thinking of places near you which you may not have previously considered:

☐ Another parish dedicated to the same patron saint as your own parish. Such a pilgrimage may result in a link-up between the two parishes on other occasions, and if the two areas are very different, this could be especially valuable.

☐ The oldest place of worship in your Diocese.

☐ The newest place of worship in your Diocese.

☐ Your cathedral.

☐ A monastery or priory, either 'working' or in ruins.

☐ A place of beauty, such as a lakeside, hillside or headland.

ACTIVITIES

ROUTE PLANNING

Once the destination has been chosen, collect together as much material as possible for the group to work with. Have a selection of tourist maps and walkers' maps (4cm to 1 km) together with any brochures or information which may come in handy for route planning:

☐ The names of churches along the way, with names and addresses of clergy who may be able to hire out a church hall for a night.

☐ Any youth hostels *en route*, together with YHA information.

☐ Information about places of interest which may be worth visiting during the pilgrimage.

> Help the group to work out distances and plan the best possible route for each stage of the journey, noting down the names of each place visited, the possibilities for accommodation and/or refreshment, and map references for the route.

The next stage is to contact people along the route who may be able to help with accommodation. A friendly, courteous letter needs to be produced within the group which can serve as a model for all the letters to be sent.

BROCHURE DESIGN

This brochure will need to include information about the destination, the aim, the cost and the date of the pilgrimage, together with a simplified route map, list of necessary equipment, type of accommodation provided and approximate distances to be covered each day, so that everyone has a clear idea of what they are letting themselves in for. Attractive cover design is also important, and should reflect the theme of the pilgrimage (see

Thinking Things Out). The printing and paper costs need to be worked out too.

This may appear a lot to do, but young people are well used to problem-solving in groups as part of their education at school, and they are likely to have a good many interesting and unusual ideas to incorporate into the brochure once the basic idea is made clear to them.

TRAIL BLAZING

Since the pilgrimage will involve some map reading, it is an excellent idea if as many of the group as possible take part in some basic map reading training. Experts from outside could be asked to come in on this — possibly from the parish Scout or Guide groups. Once people are finding their way with a reasonable degree of accuracy, try to arrange for a trail blazing day in which the entire route is checked by different groups, so that although each individual has only walked a small section in advance, the whole pilgrimage trail has been blazed. On such a day, groups take note of any difficulties or surprises, check distances covered and time spent on each stretch, and generally gather useful information.

BANNER MAKING

This banner will be carried throughout the whole of the journey, so it needs to be weatherproof, sturdy and light! Rather than just announcing the origin of the walkers, it can be a witness to the theme of Spiritual Pilgrimage, so that those who see it are given food for thought. Try out lots of designs first on paper until everyone is happy that the banner proclaims the right message, and try constructing it out of different coloured nylon fabric which is lightweight and dries quickly. Use strong thread for all stitching, and don't be tempted to rely on glue — sewing will last better, and the banner needs to look as good at the end as at the beginning.

FOOD FOR THE JOURNEY

Invite a nutrition expert to come and help some of the group plan for healthy snacks and meals along the way, and try some of these out in advance!

FIRST AID AND FITNESS

The more young people who are able to administer effective first aid the better, so this is a good opportunity to have some basic first aid sessions, with particular attention to the kind of first aid that may be needed on the walk. Preventative care is also worth practising, along with fitness training to get those muscles in good shape. Perhaps the exercises could be written up in the parish magazine or handout so that everyone can get fit!

SESSION ONE

Setting off

THINKING THINGS OUT
Have ready a long strip of plain wallpaper or lining paper which stretches all along the length of one wall if possible. On the paper is drawn in thick felt tip pen, the route of a journey, rather like this:

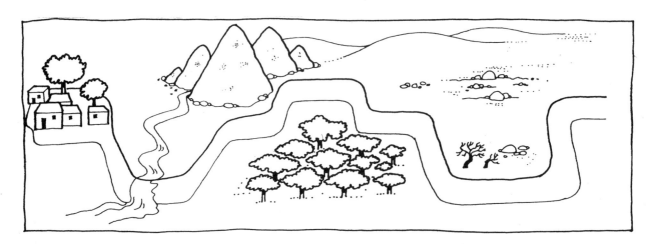

It is better if it doesn't just go in a dead straight line. This route will be referred to for every session of Thinking Things Out, so if possible it needs to stay on the wall, growing session by session, for the whole unit.

Split into small groups of three or four, and give each group a set of cards with these words written on:

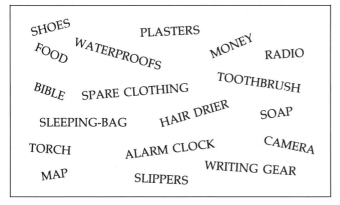

SHOES   PLASTERS
FOOD WATERPROOFS   MONEY   RADIO
BIBLE   SPARE CLOTHING   TOOTHBRUSH
SLEEPING-BAG   HAIR DRIER   SOAP
TORCH   ALARM CLOCK   CAMERA
MAP   SLIPPERS   WRITING GEAR

Also provide each group with a backpack.

1 Imagine you are setting out on a pilgrimage. Which things will you pack? Number the items in order of importance and pack them in the backpack. Then compare your order of importance with those of the other groups.

2 Now you are told there is a restriction on your luggage, and as a group you must choose only THREE items. Which will you choose and why?

To read together: Genesis 12:1-6.

3 What did Abram take with him on his journey?

4 Find out where Haran is and work out how far it is from there to Canaan. How long do you think it might have taken them?

5 What do we need to set off on our pilgrimage to heaven? Read Ephesians 6:14-18 to give you some ideas.

Draw a backpack and a person setting off on a pilgrimage to heaven, with clothing labelled. Stick this drawing at the start of the journey line.

WORSHIP

Gather in a circle round a globe and sing together *Shalom* (HOAN).

Reader 1 Matthew 2:1-2.
When Jesus had been born at Bethlehem in Judaea during the reign of King Herod, some wise men from a country in the east came into Jerusalem asking,

Reader 2 'Where is the new-born king of the Jews? We saw the rising of his star, and have come here to pay our respects.'

All Lord, guide us on our journey to find you.

Reader 3 After their interview with Herod they left, and the star whose rising they had witnessed now moved in front of them until it stopped over the place where the child was.

All Lord, guide us on our journey to find you.

Reader 1 They were overjoyed to see the star, and, having come into the house, they saw the child with Mary, his mother. Falling to their knees they honoured him with great reverence. Then, from their treasures, they offered him gifts of gold, frankincense and myrrh.

Sing together a worship chorus, such as
Majesty, worship his majesty (HOAN)
Jesus, can I tell you what I know (MSOTS)
He is Lord (HOAN)
Hosanna, hosanna (SOF4)

All Send us out into the world in peace,
to live and work
to your praise and glory. Amen.

SESSION TWO
Finding the way

THINKING THINGS OUT

In small groups of four or five people, look through the resource material you provide (a Bible; a photo of parents, labelled 'Mum and Dad'; adverts; hockey/football boots; make-up; Visa card; cigarette packet labelled 'habits'; a flower; blank video tape.)

1 Sort the material into two lots — one lot which helps us find our way on our spiritual journey through life, and the other lot which hinders us.

2 Put the helpful lot in order of importance to you as a Christian. See how each member of the group finds different things helpful. Come together as a full group now. Have ready a number of situations written out on cards and put in a box. Each sub-group is given an identity and argues their case in the situation which is drawn. Here are some ideas; you may well choose different ones which are particularly relevant to this group:

☐ A £5000 legacy has been left to the parish. How should it be spent so as to be in accordance with the 'way' of Christ?

☐ Sub-groups here may be the Catechists/Sunday school teachers; the prayer and praise group; the youth group; the local hospital/hospice; CAFOD/Action Aid/Christian Aid.

☐ The local council is thinking of opening a 'halfway house' for those recently released from prison. They have chosen a site in an attractive and expensive housing area.

Possible sub-groups may be: local residents' association; prisoners' welfare group; estate agents; local infant school; parish church.

☐ A homeless family is squatting in a derelict house in the neighbourhood.

Possible sub-groups may be: the local council; unemployed builders; the homeless family; the parish church.

Aim to air grievances, show different points of view and come to a constructive conclusion.

To read together: Ephesians 5:1-2; Hebrews 13:1-6.

3 How do these words link with the constructive suggestions offered in our role plays? On the wall map write THE WAY OF LOVE and paste on pictures of different needs and help being given.

WORSHIP

Gather again in a circle around a globe and sing together *Ubi Caritas* (SOTS 3) letting the singing fade into a time of silence.

Reader 1 John 13:12-17.
When Jesus had washed their feet, and put his coat back on, he went and settled down with them again.

Reader 2 He said to them, 'Do you understand what I have done to you? You call me Lord and Teacher, and rightly so, because that is what I am. If I, then, as your Lord and Teacher, washed your feet, you must wash the feet of one another. I have set you an example, for you to copy the way I have behaved towards you.'

All 'In all truth I tell you, no slave is more important than his master, nor any messenger more important than the one who sends him.

Reader 1 'Now that you understand this truth, how blessed you will be if you put it into practice!'

> Sing a chorus or hymn together, such as
> *A new commandment* (HOAN)
> *Peace, perfect peace* (HOAN)
> *Let there be love shared among us* (SOTS3)
> *God's Spirit is in my heart* (HOAN)

Reader 2 Lord Jesus, you are the Way;

All guide us to walk always in the path of your love. Amen.

SESSION THREE
Mountains, forests and deserts

THINKING THINGS OUT
Have a selection of pictures displayed which show very difficult terrain — rock climbers, desert, jungle, thick mud etc. Good sources for such pictures are colour supplements, exploration/outdoors or nature magazines, calendars and adventure holiday brochures.

1 In groups of two or three, tell each other about the most difficult, uncomfortable or scary journey you have ever made.

2 As one group, list some of the things that helped keep you going when times were rough. Add these to the wall 'journey' with a few of the pictures.

To read together: Isaiah 49:10.

The prophet is telling us God's promise to his people. It tells us how God promises to care for us on our spiritual journey.

3 Have you ever found you have been given help, just when you were about to give up? Were you given practical help, encouragement, appreciation or a bit of breathing space, for instance?

4 No doubt there have also been times when you have found it very hard to be a Christian. Talk about such times; you will probably be surprised to find how many of you have had similar problems.

▽

To read together: Matthew 5:10-12.

5 There! God never promised us a rose garden, or even a peaceful life, according to this reading. And he even expects us to be happy about it. List some people who have lived/are living like this. Would you be prepared to be persecuted, insulted or ridiculed for your faith, do you think?

WORSHIP

Gather in a circle round a globe and sing together *Walk with me, O my Lord* (HOAN). Let the singing fade into a time of silence.

Reader 1 Mark 13:7-13.

When you hear of wars and rumours of wars, don't be disturbed. This must all happen, but it does not mean that the end has arrived. Nation will fight against nation, and kingdom against kingdom; there will be earthquakes in some places, and famines. These are like the beginning of labour pains at a birth.

Reader 2 But you yourselves must be on your guard. You will be handed over to sanhedrins; you will be beaten in synagogues, and on my account you will be put on trial before governors and kings, so as to witness to them about me. It is first necessary for the Good News to be proclaimed to every country.

Reader 3 Lord, we pray for all who are being tortured or punished for their faith at the moment.

Silence

Reader 3 Jesus, please help them;

All give them your strength.

Reader 4 But when you are arrested and handed over, don't be anxious beforehand about what you should say; when the time comes just say whatever is then given to you, for what you say will come not from you but from the Holy Spirit.

Reader 3 Lord, we pray for the right words when we are asked about what we believe.

Silence

Reader 3 Jesus, fill us with your Spirit,

All and use us to show your love.

Sing together a chorus or song such as:
Though the mountains may fall (MSOTS)
O Lord, all the world (HOAN)
Blessed are you who are persecuted PP Vol 2)

Reader 3 Lord, in your strength
All we shall be strong. Amen.

SESSION FOUR
Food for the journey

THINKING THINGS OUT

Have a variety of food wrappers, labels and containers. Give a selection of these to each small group of two or three people.

1 Sort these foods into those that are basic to a nutritious diet, and those which are either luxury or junk food.

2 What happens to your body when it needs an intake of food — how does it let you know?

3 What happens if our bodies are deprived of the food they need?

To read together: Exodus 16:11-15; Luke 9:12-17.

4 God uses what is offered in the desert and in a lunch box, so that many thousands can be fed. What do you think the people learnt about God through being fed like this?

5 If we can only offer a little of our time/money/skills is it worth offering at all? (Look again at how many loaves and fish were offered.)

6 How does God make sure we can be regularly fed on our spiritual journey? Write any suggestions on the wall journey chart.

7 Look again at Question 3, and ask the same question about spiritual feeding.

WORSHIP

Gather in a circle round a globe and sing *Oh, come to the water* (HOAN) or *As I went a-walking one morning in Spring* (SOTS3) and let the singing fade into a time of silence.

Reader 1 John 6:33-35.

The bread of God is the bread which comes down from heaven and is giving life to the world.

All 'Sir,' they said to him, 'always give us this bread.'

Reader 2 Jesus replied, 'I am the bread of life; whoever comes to me shall never be hungry, and whoever believes in me shall never ever be thirsty.'

Sing together a chorus or song such as:
Taste and see that God is good (PP Vol. 2)
Farmer, farmer (MWTP)
Oh, how good is the Lord (HOAN)
I am the bread of life (HOAN)

Reader 1 Heavenly father, feed us on our journey

All and use us to feed others. Amen.

SESSION FIVE
Getting lost

THINKING THINGS OUT
Have some quite difficult mazes cut out of a puzzle magazine, and let everyone have a go at solving them. Do this in twos.

1 What do you have to do in a maze if you go the wrong way? Have you ever tried a full-sized maze? Tell the others about it.

2 Have you ever read the map wrongly and got yourself lost? How did you get back to the right place?

To read together: Luke 15:11-24.

3 How would you say this man had lost his way?

4 Why didn't the father just send him away, or treat him as a hired servant?

5 What can we discover about God's attitude to us when we go wrong?

To read together: Matthew 18:21-22.

6 How is Jesus suggesting we should behave to those who wrong us in any way?

7 Do you think it is possible to keep forgiving like this? How can we improve our 'stamina' in forgiving?

On the wall journey chart draw in some side roads which end in swamps or brick walls.

WORSHIP
Gather in a circle round a globe, as usual. Sing *Spirit of the living God* (HOAN) and let the singing fade into a time of silence.

Reader 1 John 14:5-6.
Thomas says to Jesus, 'Lord, we do not know where you are going, so how are we able to know the way?'

Reader 2 Jesus answers him, 'I am the Way; I am the truth and I am life. No one comes to the Father except through me.'

Reader 3 Isaiah 53:5-6.
Yet he was wounded because of our wrong-doing;
he was crushed because of our evil.
He suffered the punishment which brings us healing,
we have been made whole by the bruises he endured.

All Like sheep, we had all scattered and become lost, each wandering off our own way.

Reader 3 And the Lord laid on him the punishment

All which all of us deserved.

Sing together a chorus or hymn, such as:
Our hearts were made for you (HOAN)
O the love of my Lord (HOAN)
Talk to me (HLS)
Amazing grace (HOAN)
Lord, when I turn my back on you (HOAN)

Reader 1 Father, if we wander from your way,

All bring us back. Amen.

SESSION SIX
Journey's end

THINKING THINGS OUT
1 In small groups of two or three, tell one another how you think you might react if you were told you had only one year to live . . . what about one week . . . and one hour?

2 In what ways would your reactions be different if you were 30 years older?

To read together: Romans 8:18, 37-39.

3 Make a list of the qualities of heaven that we do know about. (The parables of the mustard seed, the yeast, the hidden treasure, and the net may help. You'll find these in Matthew 13.)

To read together: Revelation 7:13-17.

4 If we know that our life doesn't end with physical death, how does that affect our way of living?

5 How will it change the way we react when things go wrong?

6 How will it affect our willingness to suffer for our faith?

WORSHIP

Gather in a circle with the globe placed as part of the circle, rather than in the centre. Sing together *Jubilate everybody* (HOAN) and encourage dancing as well as singing.

Reader 1 1 Corinthians 13:8-10, 12.

Love never falls away. Where there are prophecies, they will come to an end; where there are tongues, they will be silent; where there is knowledge, it will vanish. For our understanding is only partial, prophesying is only partial; but once p comes, then all that is partial will con end.

Reader 2 For now we see only dim, confusing reflections in a mirror, but then we shall see face to face. Now I understand only in part, but then I shall understand fully, just as I am fully known and understood.

Sing together a chorus or hymn such as:
Our God reigns (HOAN)
Father, we love you (HOAN)
Majesty (HOAN)
God and man at table are sat down (HOAN)
Therefore the redeemed (SOF)
Jubilate everybody (SOF)

Reader 3 Father, during our pilgrimage through life prepare us for heaven,

All and welcome us into your everlasting kingdom. Amen.

GAMES

TREASURE HUNT
Work out a series of coded messages, each leading to where the next can be found. This can either be played in the confines of a building or outdoors over a specified area. Groups of three or four are given the necessary information for decoding, together with a map/chart of the area included, and the first clue. Arrange for someone to be at each stage of the journey if you are planning a route of any distance.

FOLLOW THE ROPE
This game is best played outside on fairly rough ground; if indoors, arrange the route to involve some obstacles. A rope is stretched along the route and tied at intervals — a climbing rope is ideal, though thick string also works. One by one, with a reasonable space between them, everyone is blindfolded and has to follow the route, guided by the rope or string. This can give rise to some useful discussion about the problems the blind have, and it also helps make people more aware of their other senses, apart from sight. It is also great fun!

BLOCK

One place is decided on as a 'base' and is defended by one person. During a set time everyone else scatters and hides. Their aim is to get back to base without being noticed, or 'blocked'. If the defender sees them before this happens, s/he must call out their name for them to be blocked. The best places to play this are areas which provide plenty of cover, but artificial cover could of course be provided indoors with furniture.

GAMES WITH GOALS

All the popular ball team games are to do with working together on finding a way through difficulties to reach a goal of some kind. This makes them ideal for linking with the theme of journeys. For a change from the more usual games, try giving a ball or a couple of hoops, ropes, skittles and beanbags, to groups of ten or twelve, and let them have a go at making up their own team games with a goal. Some may be worth remembering for regular use.

TRACKING

A small group sets off first to blaze the trail. The scout signs are clear and use natural materials. Stress the importance of leaving a trail that is environmentally friendly! Some time later (how long depends on the length of the trail) the others set off to be trackers. Each group of trackers needs to be small, and time must be left between each team setting out. It is a good idea to have some activity, such as cooking and eating, prepared for the finishing place, as people will all be arriving at different times, and will need something to do while they wait for the last team to arrive.

SOUVENIRS

The aim of this game is to collect a number of souvenirs from different places in the neighbourhood and be first back to base with them. Teams of five or six people are given a map of the neighbourhood, a list of the souvenirs to collect, and a colour to identify them. They are also provided with map references or crossword-type clues so that they can first work out where to find the souvenirs. They do not all have to visit each place, so part of the task is using their workforce efficiently. At each destination have the souvenirs colour-coded to be collected by the right groups.

UNIT THREE

DARKNESS AND LIGHT

AIM

To help young people explore the symbolism of darkness and light in relation to insight, perception, spiritual enlightenment, good and evil.

LENGTH OF UNIT

Six to twelve sessions.

WHAT WILL WE BE DOING?

A variety of activities, discussions, research and games which result in a 'Sound and Light' presentation using slides and a taped recording, which all the parish can learn from and enjoy.

ACTIVITIES

CANDLE-MAKING

Materials needed:
    Old candle stubs of various colours.
    Candle wax granules (from craft shops).
    Plain white household candles.
    Wicks or thin string.
    Olive oil.
    Polythene carton of sand.
    Various shaped containers for moulds.
    Old, broken wax crayons.
    Empty canned fruit or vegetable tins,
      foil dishes.
    Nightlights.

Candle-making is messy, so cover the entire area of floor and working surface with newspapers and plastic. Provide dustbin bags as aprons for candle makers. Melt the wax in foil dishes or tin cans over nightlights or a *very* low gas on a camping stove. Old candle ends can be chopped or grated to encourage faster melting. The exciting bit isexperimenting with all the different shapes and materials, as wax can be dripped or painted on, set in all kinds of containers, coloured with blobs, streaks and swirls, carved or squidged. Fix wicks in as shown, and have a selection of library books on hand to get the imaginations going.

PHOTOGRAPHY

Materials needed:
    35mm camera(s) with flash facility.
    slide film.
    blank, exposed slides.

Have a group teaching time to ensure that everyone involved knows how their camera works. Local camera club members are often very willing to help here. The aim of the group is to collect a series of slides which express the theme of darkness and light. Allow time for everyone's ideas to be jotted down, so that the group can plan the kind of shots they will go for. Obviously they will be able to take pictures of the candle-making process, and the worship provides other possibilities for candlelit faces.

Some interesting slides can be created from disused, exposed transparencies. These can be carefully scratched to make swirls and patterns of colour — perhaps to suggest fireworks or stars.

The group may want to try some set, studio shots. Hall stages may provide an opportunity for this, or even a corner of the hall, draped with material and lit with several 100 watt bulbs.

SOUND TRACK

The task of this group is to plan and record a sound track on the theme of darkness and light, using single voices, chorally read passages, original and recorded music. Naturally they will have to work closely with the photographers so as to achieve a unified whole, but within a clear framework there can be plenty of scope for individual ideas. (It won't be necessary, for instance, for every slide to relate directly to a spoken reference on the soundtrack.)

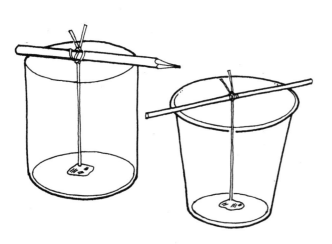

▽

23

Suggestions for Bible passages to use: Genesis 1:1-5; Exodus 13:21-22; Job 10:18-22; Job 38:12-15; Psalm 139:11-12; Isaiah 9:2-3; Isaiah 13:9-10; Matthew 4:16; John 1:1-14; John 8:12; Romans 13:11-14; 1 Peter 2:9.

The group will probably need to experiment with different effects before finalising the script. If everyone recognises this at the outset they will not think of the problems as failures, but as necessary try-outs.

SESSION ONE
Scared of the dark

THINKING THINGS OUT
Have an area of dark-blue and yellow paper on which to note down the main points raised in discussion, using yellow chalk on the dark side and blue felt-tip on the yellow side.

1 What is frightening or dangerous about the darkness?

2 Why are many children scared of the dark?

Encourage general conversation and anecdotal contributions at this stage so as to create an atmosphere which is relaxed and friendly, with no correct or incorrect answers.

Sift from the stories some of the different fears, both rational and irrational, and chalk these up on the dark-blue paper.

3 What is comforting/safe about the light?

4 In what way is light useful?
Again, encourage 'chatty' discussion, and make a note of points raised by writing them on the yellow paper.

To read together: Genesis 1:1-5 and John 1:1-5.

5 In the light (!) of what you have been talking about, what do you think the writer of Genesis was saying about the character of God?

6 Why do you think the creation story begins with total darkness being changed into light?

7 In what way/s are the two passages you have read similar?

8 How do our own discussion points about light fit in with what John wrote?

WORSHIP
Gather round in a circle, either on chairs or on the floor. If you are using the church, gather in a circle or semi-circle round the altar. Each person holds an unlighted candle. In the centre of the group, one candle is burning.

Sing together *The light of Christ* (HOAN), accompanied with instruments if you have them. Let the singing fade into a time of silence.

Reader: Genesis 1:1-5.
In the beginning God created the heavens and the earth. Now the earth was a shapeless emptiness, there was darkness over the surface of the ocean depths, and the Spirit of God breathing over the waters. God said, 'Let there be light' — and there was light. God saw that the light was good, and God separated the light from the darkness. God called the light 'day' and the darkness he called 'night'. Evening came, and morning came — the first day.

Sing together a chorus or hymn, such as:
Walk in the light (HOAN)
The light of Christ (HOAN)
Shine Jesus, shine (SOF4)
Jesus, name above all names (SOF)
Colours of day (HOAN)

During the singing, each person in turn goes and lights a candle from the central one, and places it on the floor in the centre of the group.

Reader Let us bring into the light of God's love the dark areas of our world
— those who are scared or worried
— those with no home to sleep in.

Silence

All God of love: shine in the darkness.

Reader Into his healing light we bring
— those waiting in casualty departments
— all victims of crimes and accidents.

Silence

All God of love: shine in the darkness.

Reader Into his welcoming light we bring
— those whose lives are confused
— those who are searching for life's meaning.

Silence

All God of light: shine in the darkness.

Reader John 1:1-5.

All In the beginning the Word already existed; the Word was with God and the Word was God. This Word was with God right from the beginning. Through this, everything was done; without this, not one thing that has been made could have been made. In this Word was life, and the life was the light of humankind.

And the light shines in the darkness, and the darkness has never quenched it.

Reader In the darkness of selfishness and greed, go out and shine as lights of God's love.

All In the power of our loving God, we will.

SESSION TWO
Warnings and guides

THINKING THINGS OUT
Have the last session's discussion points on display, and a sheet ready for today's points which is split into two overlapping sets, headed WARNINGS and GUIDES.

1 What different examples of warning lights can you think of?

2 What different examples of guide lights can you think of?

Discuss where the two overlap and write all the suggestions in appropriate places on the sheet.

To read together: Isaiah 9:2, Matthew 11:2-6, John 8:12-13.

3 In fours, imagine that two of you are strict Pharisees and the other two are followers of Jesus. What things in Jesus' character and behaviour have convinced you that he is the light of the world? Try to show the Pharisees that Jesus is the light they have been waiting for.

4 Look again at how some 'guide' lights also become effective 'warning' lights. How does God's light sometimes become a warning light for us?

5 What if God's light shows up areas of our life we prefer to keep dark? What *might* we do? What *should* we do?

6 Why did the Pharisees see Jesus' light as a threat?

WORSHIP
Gather round as before, holding unlit candles, and with one lit candle in the centre. Sing a chorus together such as *Do not be afraid* (HOAN), accompanied with instruments if you have them. Let the singing fade into a time of silence.

3 Readers together Isaiah 9:2-3.
The people who were walking in darkness have seen a great light.
On those living in a land of deep shadow, brilliant light has dawned.
You have enlarged the nation, O Lord, and deepened their joy.

> Sing together one of these hymns:
> *Earthen vessels* (SOTS)
> *Father, we love you* (SOTS3, HOAN)
> *Bless the Lord, my soul* (SOTS)
> *Jesus, can I tell you what I know?* (MSOTS)
>
> During the singing, each person in turn goes and lights a candle from the central one, and places it on the floor in the centre of the group.

Reader Let us bring into the light of God's love some of the dark areas of our world:
— those whose lives are in danger
— those who are imprisoned or exiled.

All God of light: shine in the darkness.

Silence

Reader Into his healing light we bring
— those undergoing surgery
— any people in pain at the moment.

Silence

All God of light: shine in the darkness

Reader Into his welcoming light we bring
— those who have lost their way
— all who have difficult decisions to make.

Silence

All God of light: shine in the darkness.

Reader 1 Matthew 11:2-6.
Now John the Baptist, who was in prison, heard about what Christ was doing, and sent two of his own disciples to ask him,

All 'Are you the One whose coming was promised, or should we be expecting someone else?'

Reader 2 Jesus answered them, 'Go back and report to John what you hear and see — blind people can see again, the lame ones are able to walk about, those with skin diseases are cleansed, and the deaf are hearing; dead people are being brought to life and the poor are personally given the good news.

All 'What blessings there are for those who do not think of me as a stumbling block!'

Readers 1 and 2 Jesus is the light of the world.

All We will walk in his light.

SESSION THREE
The darkness of evil

THINKING THINGS OUT

Have the last two sessions' discussion points on display. Have ready a selection of current newspapers, scissors and gluesticks. In twos or threes everyone cuts out several headlines, pictures or advertisements which tell stories of hate, greed, destruction, misery or deprivation in our world. These are all stuck on to a large sheet or roll of paper in a close-packed, random collage.

1 What different areas of 'darkness' have we collected?

2 Try to get behind the actual crime committed to see the spiritual darkness, or sin, that made such evil possible. (For example, in a case of violent robbery, might it be greed? influence of videos? poor upbringing? mental illness? selfishness?)

To read together: Job 14:1-2 and Psalm 130:1-4.

3 Is it possible to become better people through our own efforts?

4 How does it help if God is prepared to forgive us?

5 What else does God offer us to lighten the darkness?

To read together: John 14:15-16; John 14:27; Matthew 11:28; Galatians 5:19-25.

Stick the outline of a large cross (made of foil or shiny parcel tape) over all the depressing stories of human weakness and capacity for evil, to show how Jesus has brought the light of hope. Through his complete, all-giving love we are saved.

WORSHIP

As before, gather round in a circle or semi-circle, with one lighted candle in the centre. Sing together *Nada te turbe, nada te espante* (Taizé) and let the singing fade into a time of quietness.

Reader 1 Jeremiah 4:22.
The Lord says, 'My people are fools — they do not know me.
They are behaving childishly;
they have no understanding.
They are so smart at doing what is evil,
but useless at doing what is good.'

Reader 2 Isaiah 43:1.
But now, Israel, the Lord who created and formed you speaks to you and says,
'Do not be afraid, for I have redeemed you;
I have called you by name — you are mine.'

Sing together one of these hymns:
Come, follow me (SOTS3, HOAN)
Let there be light (SOTS3)
Jubilate everybody (SOF)
Talk to me (HLS)
During the singing, each person in turn goes and lights a candle from the central one, and places it on the floor in the centre of the group.

Reader Let us bring into the light of God's love the dark areas of our world:
— the quarrelling and heated arguments;
— all who long for revenge.

All God of light: shine in the darkness.

Silence

Reader Into his healing light we bring
— all victims of attack
— those wounded or disabled through war.

Silence

All God of light: shine in the darkness.

Reader Into his welcoming light we bring
— all who work for peace
— all who need encouragement.

Silence

All God of light: shine in the darkness.

Reader Psalm 121.

All I lift up my eyes to the mountains;
where does my help come from?
My help comes from the Lord,
who made heaven and earth.
He will not let your foot slip —
he who protects you will not fall asleep.
In fact, he who watches over Israel
never dozes or sleeps.
He is right by your side to shade you,
so that the sun will not burn you
during the day,
nor the moon during the night.
The Lord protects you from all harm,
and keeps you safe.
He will watch over all your comings and goings
both now and for ever.

Reader If the Lord is with us,

All who shall be against us!

SESSION FOUR
In the dark

THINKING THINGS OUT

As before, have all the previous discussion sheets on display, so that the 'route' so far can be traced. This time set up a sheet of card with two slits in it, and a long strip of paper which will fit through the slits comfortably.

On the strip of paper write this sentence, leaving a space between each word: 'If you want to know how to find the end of the rainbow you will have to ask the owner of the pot of gold.' Thread the paper through the card and join the ends to make a loop. It should look something like this:

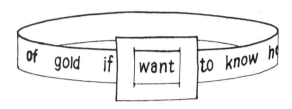

Show the card so that any one of the words is visible **except** the first or last few words. Have a few **guesses** at what the complete sentence may be. (I have **chosen** a particularly odd one so as to make it almost impossible to guess correctly!) So, we are all 'in the dark'. Show how the message gradually becomes clearer if we look at the beginning, and at the end. The more we have seen, the more chance we have of discovering the real message.

1 How many words did you need to see before you could understand the message?

To read together: Daniel 7:13-14; Micah 5:2; Isaiah 60:3; Isaiah 53:5.

2 In a way these readings are like different words in our secret message. How do they fit in with what we know of Jesus?

3 What message do you think they add up to make?

4 How was God gradually revealing this message in the many years before Jesus was born? (If you're stuck, see Romans 1:2-4.)

To read together: Acts 8:28-38.

5 In groups of three or four, think about what things Philip might have said to the Ethiopian, starting with the Isaiah passage he had been reading. If there is time, make it into a short play.

WORSHIP

Gather round as before, with a lighted candle in the centre. Sing together *Here I am, Lord* (SOTS3) and let the singing fade into a time of silence.

Reader 1 Daniel 7:13-14.

As I was gazing at this vision in the night I saw in front of me what looked like a human being, coming on the clouds of heaven. He approached the One who lives for ever and was led into his presence. To him was given authority, honour and kingly power, and the people of all nations, races and languages served him. His reign lasts for ever, it will never pass away; his kingdom will never be destroyed.

Sing together one of these songs:
Shine, Jesus, shine (SOF 4)
Ubi caritas (SOTS 3)
Our hearts were made for you (HOAN)
Therefore the redeemed (SOF)

During the singing, each person in turn goes and lights a candle from the central one, and places it on the floor in the centre of the group.

Reader 2 Let us bring into the light of God's love the dark areas of our world
— those who have never yet heard of his love
— those who live constantly in terror.

Silence

All God of love: shine in the darkness.

Reader 3 Into his healing light we bring
— those whose minds are confused by age or illness
— all those in hospital.

Silence

All God of love: shine in the darkness.

Reader 4 Into his welcoming light we bring
— the newly born;
— the newly baptised.

Silence

All God of light: shine in the darkness.

Reader 1 Mark 8:27-29.

All Jesus and his disciples went out into the villages of Caesarea Philippi. And on the way he asked his disciples, 'Who do people say I am?' 'Some say you are John the baptiser,' they answered, 'some that you are Elijah and others that you are one of the prophets.'

Reader 1 'But what about you?' he asked them. 'Who do you say I am?'

Reader 2 Peter answered him, 'You are God's anointed one — the Christ.'

Reader 1 Lord, to whom else would we go?

All You alone have the words that give eternal life.

SESSION FIVE

Quality lightbulbs

THINKING THINGS OUT

Have all the discussion points from previous sessions on display, and briefly draw attention to them. One of today's sheets is the shape of an enormous lamp bulb, cut out of very bright paper; the other is made like a blind, with a pullcord stuck at the bottom.

1 In twos or threes, talk about what you have seen in some people which has made you want to know Jesus better.

2 Now talk about the kind of behaviour which gives you a bad impression of Christians.

To read together: Matthew 5:14-16.

3 Write up on the lightbulb the qualities which you have found shining Christians have. Write on the blind the qualities which turn you or your friends away from Jesus.

4 What qualities did Jesus say would bring lasting blessing (or happiness)? You may need to read Matthew 5:1-12; John 13:34-35.

5 Why do you think real loving often involves getting hurt?

6 What will be the consequences if only a very few people shine with Christ's light in our world?

WORSHIP

Have everyone grouped as before, with a lighted candle in the centre. Sing together a chorus such as *Freely, freely* (HOAN) and let the singing fade into a time of shared peace and quietness.

Reader 1 Matthew 5:14-15.
You are the light of the world. It is impossible for a city situated on a hill to be concealed; nor would you light a lamp and put it under a bowl, but on the lampstand where it will give light to everyone in the house.

> Sing together a song or chorus such as:
> *The Spirit lives to set us free* (HOAN)
> *Open our eyes, Lord* (HOAN, SOF)
> *He is Lord!* (SOF, HOAN)
> *I will sing, I will sing* (HOAN)
>
> During the singing, each person in turn goes and lights a candle from the central one, and places it on the floor in the centre of the group.

Reader 3 Let us bring into the light of God's love
— the wasted opportunities for showing care
— the selfishness which blocks God's channels of love.

Silence

All God of love: shine in the darkness.

Reader 4 Into his healing light we bring
— the prejudiced and resentful
— those in pain which is wearing them down.

Silence

All God of love: shine in the darkness.

Reader 5 Into his welcoming light we bring
— the disillusioned and disappointed;
— those driven from Christ by unhelpful Christian witness.

Silence

All God of light: shine in the darkness.

Reader 1 Happy are those whose greatest desire is to do what God requires;

All God will satisfy them fully!

Reader 2 Jesus is the light of the world.

All We will walk in his light!

SESSION SIX
Walk in the light

THINKING THINGS OUT

Once again, display the discussion points from previous sessions. Today's sheet has a pair of closed eyes drawn in the middle of a blank face shape.

In twos, have one person blindfold and the other seeing. Each seeing person takes her/his partner on a walk around the area, negotiating doors, stairs, obstacles etc. As they walk, the 'blind' person is told where s/he is, what things look like, what the colours are and so on. Allow about 10 minutes for this.

1 How did the blindfolded ones feel during the walk? (Scared? Vulnerable? Dependent? Grateful for help? Frustrated/resentful?)

2 How did it feel when the blindfold was taken off? (Sense of relief/gratitude/surprise?)

3 Have you ever felt frustrated because someone else couldn't 'see' what you meant about something important?

To read together: Mark 8:22-25.

4 How do you think the blind man felt — when he saw people looking like trees? — when he saw clearly?

5 Between you, make a list of four or five situations you have heard/seen/read about, where you feel people have 'blinded' themselves to what is right and just. (Perhaps through prejudice, revenge, injustice or nationalism.)

6 How can we encourage people to take their blindfolds off?

7 Are we walking around 'blindfolded' ourselves? See if you can recognise any prejudices in yourselves, and pull those blindfolds off now!

WORSHIP

Once again, have everyone grouped in a circle, with a lighted candle in the centre. Sing together *Open our eyes, Lord* (SOF) and let the singing fade into a time of quietness.

Reader 1 Ephesians 5:8-9.
It is true that you used to be darkness, but now, as the Lord's people, you are light. So you must walk as children of light, because light produces fruit of all goodness and truth.

> Sing together a hymn or chorus such as:
> *The Spirit lives to set us free* (HOAN)
> *More love, more power* (SOF4)
> *Shine, Jesus, shine* (SOF4)
> *Colours of day* (HOAN)
>
> During the singing, each person lights a candle and brings it back to her/his place, so that there is a circle of light.

Reader 2 Lord, help us
to remove all blindness and prejudice
from our hearts.

All God of light, enlighten our lives.

Reader 3 Lord, give us courage
to walk in your light
and live in your love.

All God of light, enlighten our lives.

Reader 4 Lord, we ask you
for clearer vision
to see you and know you
more and more.

All God of light, enlighten our lives.

Reader 1 The light shines in the darkness,

All and the darkness has never put it out.

GAMES

WOLVES

Two people go out of the room while the others find somewhere to hide. The lights are turned off and the door opened a crack to let the two wolves in. When the door is shut again the wolves howl and walk round trying to find the others in the room. When they are found they join the wolves until it seems as if everyone has been discovered.

The lights are turned on and if anyone is still undiscovered, he or she is the winner.

BLINDFOLD OBSTACLE COURSE

One person goes outside while the others set up an obstacle course. The outsider is then blindfolded and taken to the start of the course. The others sit round the edge of the course and have to guide the blindfolded person by giving instructions (e.g. Take two steps sideways to your right. Now crawl forward, keeping low.) See if it is possible to get right through the course without touching any of the obstacles. Then change the course for the next volunteer.

One intriguing variation is to make one course completely empty of obstacles, but still give instructions as if the obstacles were there. How does the volunteer feel on looking back over what s/he thought was filled with hazards but was in fact perfectly safe?

SHIPS THAT PASS IN THE NIGHT

Split the group into two. The two halves start at opposite ends of the hall. Their aim is to get as many as possible to the other end of the hall without being taken by the other group. Of course, each group is also aiming to intercept as many as possible of their opponents, taking them as prisoners. The lights are put out as soon as everyone is ready to start, and put on again when the groups have swapped ends. If anyone is touched by the opposing group, they must 'come quietly'. The stealthier the group, the more successful they will be!

INTERROGATION

A group of four or five people plan a crime, and decide on one member who is the culprit. Then everyone sits round a central chair, which is spotlighted (as in Mastermind). The group tells the others what crime has been committed and then each member in turn is spotlit and questioned, to try and discover who the culprit is. After the questions, the 'jury' take a vote on who they think the culprit is, and the true culprit makes him- or herself known.

PIRATES' TREASURE

This is a game for playing outside in the dark, but could be adapted for use indoors if necessary. Split into small groups of four or five people — at least three groups are needed. One group is in possession of the treasure, which should be quite bulky and heavy. (Two buckets full of stones, for instance.) These pirates are taken to their position in the centre of the area of play, and their task is to get themselves and their treasure to a point marked on a map or chart. The other groups are taken to their places. Their aim is to intercept the pirates with treasure, steal the booty and get it intact to the specified point.

All groups will need a chart or map, torches and lengths of coloured wool tied round their arms. Once this wool has been pulled off, the person has lost his or her life and can no longer take part actively, though watching and accompanying are still allowed.

SHADOWS

Hang a washing line across one end of a hall, or between two trees outside, and peg a double sheet on it. (Pale colours are best.) Put a bright light about 2 metres behind the sheet and play some music everyone likes dancing to or clowning around to. One, two or three at a time go and dance, or make shadow actions behind the sheet. Keep lights low in the rest of the hall, or wait till dusk if outside. Once a few people have broken the ice in this it quickly becomes hilarious!

UNIT FOUR

GREEN

AIM
To explore the wonder and variety of God's creation, and discover from it more about the character of the creator.

LENGTH OF UNIT
Six to twelve sessions.

WHAT WILL WE BE DOING?
Establishing a 'God's Acre' — a conservation garden which will be for the benefit of all those living in the parish.

ACTIVITIES
PLANNING A GARDEN
The first important task is to choose a suitable site. It can be quite small and would, ideally, be close to the church. Naturally, it is essential that group leaders choose the site, ask for and obtain permission for the garden before this unit is introduced! In many cases, parishes would be only too pleased to have some untidy corner cared for and put to good use, but it is always as well to check first.

Take everyone round to view the site and then let everyone have a go at drawing a plan of how it might look when complete. The plans can be discussed and any good suggestions included in a final plan, made to scale. You could invite a local natural history expert to come in on this planning stage to offer advice. Have plenty of wildlife books available as well, so that the garden is planned to provide suitable accommodation for the plants and animals you hope will live there.

CLEARING THE SITE
This will be different for every site, but will usually involve getting rid of a considerable amount of rubbish! See if there is anything which could be used later on or recycled and avoid getting rid of any existing wild plants; in other words, work with what you have, rather than starting completely from scratch.

ESTABLISHING A POND
A natural pond is a valuable resource for many creatures and should be quite shallow at one end to allow safe access for smaller animals and birds. Having dug to the required depth and width, you need to smooth off the area, put down a layer of newspapers and then lay the pond lining material — heavy duty black polythene works well. Ensure that the entire area is thoroughly covered so as to keep the water in. The local library will have some useful books about pond-making, and garden centres are also helpful. As a general rule, don't rush; each stage needs time to settle, and evolve naturally. Once the pond is well balanced it will look after itself and inmates will thrive.

PLANTING
Since this is a natural garden, we shall be introducing plants which enjoy the conditions we have. It is both fun and useful for the group to test the soil and then research for suitable plants. Bear in mind which plants attract butterflies and birds, which provide ground cover and protection, and which provide food. Packets of mixed wild flower seeds are available, but need to be used with care, as they often contain varieties which may quickly engulf your garden! Again, have a good selection of information books, pamphlets and magazines for the group to use in making their choices.

NATURE WATCH
Even heavily built-up areas hold possibilities for a nature watch. You may not have woodland or coast nearby, but there may well be a canal or river, a piece of wasteland or a park, all of which can be surprisingly full of wildlife and well worth watching. Take a few pocket books to refer to and try collecting sketches of every different leaf, and every different creature seen, including all the obvious ones we tend to take for granted. If people work in groups of four or five, they can compare their findings with those of other groups at the end of the watch. Set a time limit and make sure that each group has a reliable way of knowing the time.

INFORMATION SHEET
Once the garden is beginning to be established, others in the parish would find an information sheet or notice useful. This could also be displayed in the local library, as the garden could be a resource for other groups and schools. The sheet needs to be informative and friendly, with plenty of drawings (both 'straight' and cartoons). It should include something about the appearance and habits of plants and animals likely to use the garden, together with the story of how the garden was made.

SESSION ONE
Making a garden

THINKING THINGS OUT

Give each person a small lump of modelling clay. Have a stop-watch or cooking timer ready.

1 In exactly two minutes, create an animal. Are you ready? GO! Put all the animals where they can be seen by everyone.

2 God made us in his likeness; like him, we are CREATIVE as you can definitely see! Now each take an animal made by someone else, and in exactly one minute, jot down anything the model suggests to you about the character and talents of its maker. (This need not be too serious, of course.) Put the models back on show with their lists, and see if they got anywhere near the truth about the makers!

To read together: Genesis: 1:9-13.

3 How do you think God might have felt about his creation? How do you feel when you know you have done your best, and have made a good job of something?

To read together: Genesis 2:4b-9.

4 This is an older creation story. How is it different from the first story we read?

5 What can we find out about God's character from reading these creation stories? Make a list of what you have discovered, writing the qualities on a chart, like this:

WORSHIP

At the centre of the circle have an arrangement of natural materials linked with earth, such as soil and stones, clay pots, plants and seeds, nuts and berries. Gather around this and sing *Morning has broken* (HOAN), letting the singing fade into a time of silence.

Reader 1 Genesis 1:26-31.
  Then God said, 'Let us make people in our own image and in our own likeness, and let them be in charge of the fish of the sea, and the birds of the sky, and over all the living creatures that move along the ground.'

Reader 2 So God created humankind in the image of himself; in the image of God he created it, male and female he created them. God blessed them and said to them, 'Be fertile and have many children, fill the earth and tame it. Be responsible for the fish of the sea, the birds of the sky and all the living creatures that move along the ground.'

Reader 1 Then God said, 'Look, I am giving you every seedbearing plant on the surface of the earth, and every tree with seedbearing fruit. They will be food for you. And to all the wild animals, all the birds of the sky and every living creature which creeps on the ground — to them I give all the foliage for their food.' And so it was.

All God looked at everything he had made, and he was well pleased with it.

Sing together a hymn or chorus, such as:
Praise the Lord (HOAN)
All the nations of the earth (HOAN)
He's got the whole world (HOAN)
Oh Lord, all the world belongs to you (HOAN)

Reader 1 Lord, you made us responsible for your world;

All make us wise and careful, so that we look after it well. Amen.

SESSION TWO
Rainbows

THINKING THINGS OUT
While the last part of Britten's *Noyes Fludde* is being played, give each small group a Bible and a quick timed quiz on the story. Here is the quiz. (Answers found in Genesis 6:9-9:17.)

> 1 What were the names of Noah's sons?
>
> 2 Why was God going to destroy everyone?
>
> 3 What measurements was the boat to have?
>
> 4 What was Noah to take into the boat?
>
> 5 Why was God willing to spare Noah from destruction?
>
> 6 How long were they in the boat before the flood came?
>
> 7 How long did the flood last?
>
> 8 Which creature was the first to find land?
>
> 9 Where did the boat come to rest?
>
> 10 What date is given for when the ground was completely dry again?

Give everyone a time limit (5 minutes?) and then share the answers in the full group.

To read together: Genesis 9:8-15.

1 What was the first thing that Noah did when he touched dry land again? Why did he do this, do you think?

2 The rainbow is the sign of a promise; what is the promise?

3 What qualities does God show in the story of the flood? Are any characteristics mentioned last time reinforced by this story? List your findings on the chart in a different colour.

WORSHIP
Gather round an arrangement of natural material on the theme of water, with sand, shells, stones etc arranged on a mirror. Sing *Do not be afraid* (HOAN), and let the singing fade into a time of silence.

Reader Genesis 9:16-17.
> When the rainbow appears in the clouds, I shall see it and remember the everlasting covenant between God and all the living creatures of every kind on the earth. So God told Noah, 'That is the sign of the Covenant I have established between me and all the living things on earth.'

All The oceans lift up their voice, O Lord, they lift up their voice in a roar of pounding waves.
Yet mightier than the ocean's roar, and more powerful than its pounding waves is the almighty Lord who rules over all (Psalm 93).

> Sing together a chorus or hymn such as:
> *Listen, let your heart keep seeking* (HOAN)
> *Send forth your Spirit, O Lord* (HOAN)
> *Father we love you* (HOAN)

Reader Father, creator, we thank you for your world;

All help us to work with you and not against you. Amen.

SESSION THREE
Power

THINKING THINGS OUT
Give everyone a minute to jot down as many different creatures as possible.

Share ideas in the full group so as to see the great variety and abundance of life on this planet.

To read together: Psalm 139:13-18.

1 Although God has created such vast quantities and varieties, what does this reading tell us about his attitude to each particular person?

2 What does it mean to know someone really well? How many people do you know really well?

3 Do you ever feel you don't even know yourself completely?

To read together: Matthew 10:29-31

4 If God is that concerned about each one of millions of creatures, how would he like us to treat them, do you think?

▽

5 Make a list of five or six ways we could put this into practice in our world.

> ADVANCE NOTICE
> Ask some people to bring the following for next session's 'Thinking Things Out':
> A small caged pet (hamster, gerbil or mouse).
> A plant in flower.
> Vegetables and fruit.

WORSHIP

Gather round in a circle, with a display of different leaves, flowers or rocks and minerals in the centre. Sing either *If I were a butterfly* (HOAN) or *O Lord my God* (HOAN) and let the singing fade into a time of silence.

Reader 1 Psalm 36:5-9.

Your constant love, O Lord, reaches to the heavens;
your faithfulness to the skies.

Reader 2 Your righteousness towers like the great mountains; your justice is deep as the seas.

All In your care both people and animals are safe.

Reader 1 How precious, O Lord, is your unfailing love!
Both great and small find refuge under the shadow of your wings.

Reader 2 We feast on the abundant food you provide for us;
you give us drink from your river of refreshment and joy.

All For you are the fountain from which all life springs,
and in your light we can see light.

> Sing together a chorus or hymn, such as:
> *Sing to the mountains* (SOTS)
> *Let the mountains dance* (MWTP)
> *Rejoice in the Lord always* (HOAN)
> *How great is our God* (HOAN)

Reader 1 Let everything in all creation

All praise the Lord, our God! Amen.

SESSION FOUR

In particular

THINKING THINGS OUT

Make sure that every small group of two or three people has a plant or flower, a small (caged) pet, such as a gerbil or hamster, or a vegetable or piece of fruit.

1 Have a close look at your animal or plant and write down as many different things as you notice about it in the time allowed. Set the timer for five or ten minutes. Are you ready? ... GO!

2 In the full group, share all the things you noticed, about all the different plants and animals.

To read together: Job 40:15-24.

3 Here is another creature who has been closely observed! What do you think he is? (He has a different name now.)

4 What characteristics of God the creator can we add to our list in the light of the plants and animals we have studied? Write them in on the chart in a different colour.

WORSHIP

Gather round in a circle, with some of the creatures and plants in the centre. Sing *All the nations of the earth* (HOAN) and let the singing fade into a time of silence.

Reader 1 Psalm 33:4-7, 22.

For the word of God is eternal,
full of truth and constancy;
he will delight in what is right and just.

All Earth is full of his faith and love.

Reader 2 By his word the sky was created,
when he spoke the stars shone out;
water he gathered into lakes and seas;
with treasure he filled the ocean depth.

All May your constant love be with us, O Lord,
as we place our hope in you.

> Sing together a chorus or hymn, such as:
> *He's got the whole world* (HOAN)
> *O the love of my Lord* (HOAN)
> *Open our eyes, Lord* (SOF 4)
> *Come into the holy of holies* (SOF 4)

Reader 3 Praise the Lord from the earth,
you vast sea monsters and ocean depths;
you lightning and hail, snow and clouds,
you stormy winds that obey his command.

Reader 4 Praise him, you mountains and all you hills,
fruit trees and cedar trees,
wild animals and cattle,
all you small creatures and flying birds,

All praise the Lord! Amen.

SESSION FIVE
Thinking big

THINKING THINGS OUT

If it happens to be dark and a clear night, begin with a star-gaze outside. Look for one or two easily identified constellations, or simply have everyone count how many stars they can see.

If it isn't dark and/or clear, have ready either a set of slides or a selection of books and pictures of the universe, and the night sky from earth.

[1] In small groups, discuss what you have seen and see if between you, you can name all the planets in our solar system, or draw any of the star constellations.

To read together: Psalm 8:3-9.

[2] Why was the psalmist surprised to find God had bothered with human beings?

[3] What can we discover about God by looking at the universe he has made? List your ideas in a new colour on the chart.

[4] Do you think that we ought to accept any responsibility for the care of the universe, or should our responsibilities stay with our own planet?

[5] Would it change your ideas about God and Jesus if life were discovered on another planet? If so, how?

To read together: Romans 8:38-39.

WORSHIP

Gather round in a circle, with a picture of one of the planets in the centre. Sing together *Adoramus te, domine* (Taizé) (SOTS) and let the singing fade into a time of silence.

Reader 1 Psalm 29:3-4.
> The voice of the Lord is heard in the waters;
> the God of glory thunders
> and his voice reverberates over the oceans
> in all its power and majesty.

Reader 2 Psalm 104:1-5.
> O Lord, my God, how great you are!
> you are clothed with splendour and majesty,
> you wrap yourself in light.
> You spread out the heavens like a tent
> and build your home above the waters,
> You make the clouds your chariot
> and ride on the wings of the wind.
> You make the winds your messengers
> and flames of fire your servants.

All The Lord is good; his love is eternal.

Sing together a chorus or hymn such as:
He is Lord (HOAN)
Hosanna! to the king of kings (SOF4)
Put your hand in the hand (Alleluya!)
Oh Lord, all the world belongs to you (HOAN)

Reader 3 The Lord is good;
All his love is eternal. Amen.

SESSION SIX
Positively green

THINKING THINGS OUT

[1] In small groups of two or three people, see if you can think of five ways that humans have tried to protect and improve the environment during the last ten years.

[2] In the full group, swap and share your ideas; you may be agreeably surprised at how much is done now compared with ten years ago.'

[3] Do you think it is possible for any good to come out of environmental disasters? Try to give examples of what has been learnt from our mistakes.

[4] In some areas there is still much to be done. What is your reaction when you hear of dismal prospects for the future of our environment?

To read together: Luke 8:22-25.

[5] What conclusions would you draw from this story about Jesus? (He is in control.)
To read together: Matthew 24:29-30; 36-39.

[6] What does Jesus suggest about the end of the world as we know it?

[7] How might this affect the way we live in the present?

WORSHIP

Gather round in a circle, with a globe and candles in the centre. Sing *Jesus, remember me* (Taizé) (SOTS3) and let the singing fade into a time of silence.

Reader 1 Genesis 3:17-19.

To the man God said, 'Because you listened to your wife and ate from the tree from which I had forbidden you to eat, cursed is the soil because of you! Through painful toil you will get food from it as long as you live. It will produce brambles and thistles as you eat the plants of the land. By the sweat of your brow you will work for your food until you return to the ground, just as you were taken from it.

All 'For you are dust, and to dust you will return.'

Reader 2 1 Corinthians 15:20-22.

However, Christ has in fact been raised from death, the first fruit of all those who have fallen asleep in death. For since it was through a man that death began, so it is through a man that the dead are raised to life. Just as in Adam all die,

All so in Christ shall all be brought to life.

> Sing together a chorus or hymn, such as:
> *Sing to the mountains* (SOTS)
> *Jubilate everybody* (SOF)
> *Tell out my soul* (HOAN)
> *Shine, Jesus, shine* (SOF4)

Reader 3 Jesus is Lord of all.

All His life sets our lives free.

GAMES

SURVIVAL
This game shows the natural balance of needs, resources and animal populations. Have a chart or OHP to record results at each go. Divide the group equally into two lines who stand facing each other at each end of the room. At one end of the room are the mice, with their needs of water, food and shelter; at the other end of the room are the resources they need. Tell everyone the hand signs for the resources:

FOOD

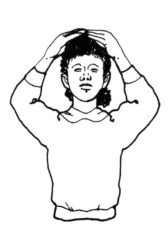

SHELTER

WATER

36

First, the two lines turn their backs on each other, and each mouse decides on a need, making the appropriate hand sign. At the same time, each of those in the other line decides on what resource to provide, and makes the appropriate hand sign.

When the leader says so, the two lines turn to face each other and walk slowly towards one another. A mouse showing his need for shelter, for instance, must try to find someone from the other line who offers shelter; a mouse needing food must link up with someone offering food, and so on. If a mouse fails to find the resource he needs, he joins the resource line. If a resource fails to be needed, she stays in the resource line. If a mouse manages to find the resource he needs, he takes the resource back with him to become another mouse! If anyone runs forward instead of walking, they get shot by the farmer, and are out of the game.

The process is repeated, and the results of numbers in the lines are plotted on the chart each time, until the natural balance of nature can be seen.

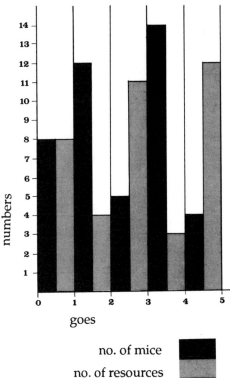

no. of mice
no. of resources

WHAT CREATURE AM I?
The name or picture of a creature is worn on the back of a volunteer, and shown to everyone in the group. The 'creature' then asks questions of everyone in turn, so as to find out what s/he is. Questions can only be answered YES or NO.

NATURE/POLLUTION TRAIL
Either use an existing trail near by, if there happens to be one, or create one of your own — a garden, park, or even town centre safari. Walk round taking note of every plant and animal, but also of every environmental hazard and pollution zone. Duplicate leaflets for people to follow the trail; if you find bad pollution problems, why not invite your local M.P. to follow the trail with you?

RIVER CROSSING
You won't necessarily need a real river; any muddy ditch will do. If you don't even have a muddy ditch, designate a stretch of ground which is going to be the 'river'! The idea is that people work together in teams to get everyone in the team safely across without getting wet (or muddy). Ropes, planks, fallen tree trunks etc. can be used.

UNIT FIVE

RICH OR POOR

AIM
To discover what it means to be rich and to be poor, spiritually as well as materially.

LENGTH OF UNIT
Six to twelve sessions (plus performances).

WHAT WILL WE BE DOING?
We will be producing a musical play about Saint Francis, who exchanged material wealth for complete poverty, and found himself richer as a result. The text, music and performing notes for *Francis!* are on pages 165-204.

ACTIVITIES

ACTING
Francis! has plenty of crowd scenes and walk-on parts which everyone can join in, and speaking/singing parts. It is designed so that one scene rolls into another, which makes it suitable for either a very simple or a more elaborate production.

If there are no potential producers among you, invite one in from the parish to work with you for this unit. This encourages liaison between different age groups in parish life, and spreads the workload. Begin with a play reading and rehearse during the time you normally meet.

MUSIC
Again, invite a guest music director if necessary, and use any musicians in the group. The music is not difficult, and many of the songs are sung by everyone.

COSTUMES
Part of the fun of the production is in creating costumes and props. Basic ideas are given, and general guidelines, but there is plenty of scope for imaginations to get exercised.

PUBLICITY
This will involve designing and creating posters and programmes, and looking at other possible sources of publicity in the area, such as local radio, and local newspapers. It is important that the public know about all the positive, challenging things young people are doing, and this provides an opportunity for such news to be spread.

WORKING WITH YOUNG CHILDREN
There are two short dances which are very effective if done by young children. Some of the group can work with children of 4-6 years, either using the dance as suggested for rain and doves, or creating their own to teach them.

SESSION ONE
Who's rich, who's poor?

THINKING THINGS OUT
Split into small groups of four or five people and give each the set of pictures for this session. Ask the groups to sort their pictures into 'RICH' and 'POOR'.

1 What made you decide which pictures were of rich people and which of poor people? Swap different ideas about this in the large group.

2 What is poverty? How many different ways of being poor can you think of?

3 Can a poor person be rich, or a rich person poor?

To read together: Luke 21:1-4.

4 In what way were the rich men actually poorer than the widow with her two copper coins?

WORSHIP
Gather in a circle and sing *Oh how good is the Lord* (HOAN). Let the singing fade into a time of silence.

Reader 1 Mark 10:17-23.
> As Jesus started out on a journey, someone came running up and knelt down in front of him, asking,

Reader 2 'Good teacher, what must I do to inherit life that lasts for ever?'

Reader 1 Jesus said to him, 'Why do you call me "good"'? Not one person is good apart from God. You know the commandments — do not commit adultery, do not commit murder, do not steal, do not give false testimony, do not cheat, honour your father and mother.'

Reader 2 But the man answered, 'Teacher, I have kept all these commandments since I was a child.'

Reader 1 Jesus looked him straight in the eye, and was filled with love for him. 'You only need to do one more thing,' he said. 'Go and sell whatever you possess and give it to the poor, and you will have treasure in heaven. And come; follow me.'

Reader 2 But the man's face fell at these words, and he went away in sadness, because he owned a great many possessions. Looking round at his disciples Jesus said, 'How difficult it will be for the wealthy to enter the Kingdom of God!'

Reader 3 Father, we ask you to make us rich;

All rich in loving care, in peace and in joy.

> Sing together a song or chorus such as:
> *Give thanks with a grateful heart* (SOF4)
> *I will sing, I will sing* (HOAN)
> *Seek ye first* (HOAN)
> *How great is our God* (SOF)

Reader 1 Happy are you poor;

All the Kingdom of God is yours! Amen.

SESSION TWO
Marching orders

THINKING THINGS OUT
In small groups of two or three work out how you might budget a weekly income of £200. Give each group a different identity; here are some ideas:

- [ ] A single person working in London and living in the suburbs.

- [ ] A family with two children, aged 5 and 2 years.

- [ ] A single parent with three children, aged 11, 8 and 6 years.

After a few minutes, exchange ideas and budgets, which should highlight needs and luxuries.

To read together: Matthew 10:7-10.

1. These were Jesus' instructions when he sent out his disciples ahead of him during his ministry on earth. Why do you think he sent them out 'poor'?

2. What might their simple, basic life-style help them to remember?

3. How do our materialistic lives draw us away from living as Christ's followers?

4. How did Francis find that poverty helped him to be 'rich'?

WORSHIP
Gather round in a circle, with some flowers and candles in the centre. Sing together *Bless the Lord, my soul* (Taizé) (SOTS3), and let the singing fade into a time of silence.

Reader 1 Psalm 127:1.
Unless the Lord builds the house,

All the work of the builders is useless;

Reader 2 unless the Lord is protecting the city,

All the sentries stand guard in vain.

> Sing together a song or chorus such as:
> *God's Spirit is in my heart* (HOAN)
> *Morning has broken* (HOAN)
> *Make me a channel of your peace* (HOAN)

Reader 3 Psalm 23.
The Lord is my shepherd; there is nothing more I need.

All He gives me rest in green meadows of grass and leads me beside calm water.

Reader 3 He renews my strength.
True to his name,
he guides me along the paths of righteousness.

All Even if I walk through the darkest valley, I shall fear no evil,

Reader 3 for you are with me;
your shepherd's rod and staff give me courage and comfort.

All You prepare a feast for me
in view of all my enemies.

Reader 3 You honour me, anointing my head with oil;
my cup is filled to overflowing.

All Surely your goodness and love
will follow me all my life,
and I will live in the home of the Lord for ever. Amen.

SESSION THREE
Satisfying needs

THINKING THINGS OUT

In small groups of two or three people, give out pieces of paper or card shaped like different pets — at least two shapes to each group.

1 On your card, make a list of whatever that particular animal needs in order to survive.

In the whole group, have a picture of a human family.

2 What do we need for survival and for quality of life?

3 Why do you think some people can survive contentedly on very little, while others are always miserable and greedy, however much they have?

4 Which of our needs as humans do you know God provides for?

To read together: Luke 12:22-31.

5 What is the one thing Jesus wants us to be concerned about?

6 If we all did this, how would people's needs start being provided for?

WORSHIP

Gather round in a circle, again with candles, flowers or driftwood. Sing *Seek ye first the kingdom of God* (HOAN) and let the singing fade into a time of reflective silence.

Reader 1 Luke 12:32-34.
> Do not be afraid, little flock, for it is your Father's pleasure to give you the Kingdom. Sell your possessions and give the money to charity. Make yourselves purses which will not wear out, and accumulate limitless wealth in heaven, where no thief will creep up on you and no moth destroys.

All For wherever your treasure is, that's where your heart will be as well.

Reader 2 Jesus said, 'Come to me, all who are weary and whose load is heavy;

All I will give you rest.'

Sing together a hymn or chorus such as:
O come to the water (SOTS3; HOAN)
Our hearts were made for you, Lord (SOTS3)
If you only knew (SOTS3)
Earthen vessels (SOTS3)

Reader 1 Lord, give us the courage to give ourselves away

All so that we have room for your riches. Amen.

SESSION FOUR
The world's poor

THINKING THINGS OUT

Have a supply of national newspapers and colour supplements/magazines available for each small group of three to four people.

1 In your small group, use the newspapers and magazines to help you fill in the chart on the resource sheet.

2 In the large group, compare charts to see everyone's ideas. The ones everybody has thought of probably show a very urgent need for help.

To read together: James 2:14-17.

3 Are we Christians sometimes a bit like this? Think of two examples where we seem to say how sorry we are, but don't actually do anything about it.

4 Now think of two examples where the Church has been happy to get involved in spite of danger or disease.

5 Where do you think the Church, as the body of Christ, should be showing a more wholehearted willingness to provide for the poor, both physically and spiritually?

WORSHIP

Gather round in a circle, with a basket containing a crust of bread and a cup of water placed in the centre of the circle. Sing *Listen, let your heart keep seeking* (HOAN) and let the singing fade into a time of silence.

Reader 1 Matthew 25:31-40.
> When the Son of Man shall come in his glory . . . then all the nations will be gathered in his presence. And he will separate them into two groups, just as the shepherd separates the sheep from the goats. He will place the 'sheep' on his right hand side and the 'goats' on his left. Then the King will say to those on his right,

Reader 2 'Come, all of you who have been blessed by my Father, receive as your inheritance the kingdom which has been prepared for you ever since the foundation of the world. For I was hungry and you gave me something to eat, I was thirsty and you gave me a drink, I was a stranger and you made me welcome, naked and you clothed me, I was ill and you looked after me, I was in prison and you came to visit me.'

Reader 1 Then the righteous will reply,

All 'Lord, when did we see you hungry and nourish you? Or thirsty and gave you a drink? When did we see you a stranger and made you welcome, or naked and we provided clothes?

And when did we see you ill, or in prison and we came to your help?'

Reader 1 The King will answer,

Reader 2 'In all truth I tell you, that whatever you did for the least of these brothers of mine, you did it for me.'

> Sing together a chorus or hymn, such as:
> *Come, follow me* (SOTS3)
> *Father, I place into your hands* (HOAN)
> *Here I am, Lord* (SOTS3)

Reader 1 Lord Jesus, fill the world with your love

All and let your will be done in us. Amen.

SESSION FIVE

Spoil yourself!

THINKING THINGS OUT

Have ready lots of different advertisements for food, useful gadgets, luxury items, medicines and cleaning agents. Distribute these among small groups of three or four people.

[1] Pick out all the advertisements which encourage us to spoil ourselves or give ourselves a treat.

[2] Pick out any advertisements which appeal to our wish to help someone close to us and make life better for them.

[3] You can probably see from the number in each group of advertisements what the advertisers have found will make us spend most money! Share your ideas about this in the full group.

To read together: 1 Timothy 6:6-8.

[4] It is part of our survival technique that we instinctively look after ourselves and our loved ones, and it is right that we do so. (Jesus advised us to care for others as much as we naturally care for ourselves. Matthew 7:12.) How can we make sure the sales pressure all around us doesn't push us into overdoing the care of oneself?

To read together: Matthew 10:8.

[5] If we know that everything we have comes from God's generosity to us, what will our attitude to possessions be?

WORSHIP

Gather round in a circle, with a bowl of money in the centre. Sing together *All that I am* (HOAN) and let the singing fade into a time of silence.

Reader 1 Matthew 13:7, 22.
In Jesus' story of the farmer who sowed the seed, some of the seed fell among thorn bushes, which grew up and choked the plants.

Reader 2 Jesus explained that the seeds that fell among thorn bushes stand for those who hear the message; but the worries about this life and the love for riches choke the message, and they don't bear fruit.

> Sing together a chorus or hymn such as:
> *Spirit of the living God* (SOTS)
> *Holy, holy, holy is the Lord* (SOTS3; HOAN)
> *Peace, perfect peace* (HOAN)
> *Peace prayer* (SOTS3)

Reader 3 Luke 6:38.
Give to others and gifts will be given to you — a full measure, pressed down, shaken together and overflowing will be poured into your lap.

All For the measure you use in giving to others, will be the same measure God uses in giving you.

Reader 3 Loving Lord, as you have freely given to us,

All may we give freely to others. Amen.

SESSION SIX
Where do we go from here?

THINKING THINGS OUT

Have available information (and some pictures, if possible) of all areas of giving that the parish is involved with. It may well come as quite a surprise to find how much giving goes on.

1 On a chart, list all the present 'help' areas, grouped as seems appropriate. (For instance, all missionary support might be in one section, education in another, health in another; it will of course vary with each parish.)

2 Are there any glaring gaps which we ought to be concerned with? If so, list these in another colour.

3 Would any area benefit from more publicity in the parish, so that more people are aware of the needs? If so, ring these in another colour, and note any suggestions made.

To read together: Mark 4:30-32.

4 God is used to starting small — he often works this way! Take one small area of your parish giving and plan to make it better.

WORSHIP

Gather round in a circle with a list of giving in the centre, surrounded with candles. Sing *God forgave my sin* (HOAN) and let the singing fade into a time of silence.

Reader 1 Matthew 5:43-48.
   You have heard that it was said, 'You shall love your neighbour and hate your enemy.' But I say this to you: love your enemies, and pray for those who persecute you, so that you may be true children of your Father in heaven.

Reader 2 After all, he makes his sun rise on both the evil and the good, and he sends rain on both the just and the unjust.

Reader 1 If you only love those who love you, what reward will you get? Don't even the tax collectors do that?

Reader 2 And if you only ever talk to your friends, how have you excelled yourself? Don't even the gentiles do that much?

Both So you must be perfect, just as your heavenly Father is perfect.

Sing together a hymn or chorus such as:
Let there be love (SOTS3)
Ubi caritas (Taizé) (SOTS3)
Shine, Jesus, shine (SOF4)

Reader 3 1 Corinthians 13:4-7.
   Love is long-suffering and kind. Love is not jealous or boastful or conceited. Love is never rude or self-seeking, nor does it easily take offence or nurse grievances. Love does not enjoy what is underhand, but takes delight in what is honest and true.

All Love works in every situation; it is always ready to trust, to hope and to persevere, whatever the difficulties.

Reader 3 Lord, increase our loving care for other people
All and may our caring draw others to know the richness of your forgiving love. Amen.

GAMES

WINNER TAKES ALL

Many card games and boxed games are based on acquiring more than anyone else in order to win. Have a session with a variety of such games going on. Then see if anyone can invent a game in which the person who manages to give most away is the winner, for a change.

MONEY SPINNER

Give everyone a set amount of money to start with (on the clear understanding that this will be given back!). Each person is given a week/month to make the money grow. See who manages to make most.

ROLL A COIN/SHOVE HA'PENNY

Draw a grid on a piece of card, with different numbers in each square. Roll or shove your coin from the edge of the card. To see what you score, look at the number the coin lands on.

COVER THE COIN

Have a bowl of water with a pound or 50p coin at the bottom. If you can drop a coin down through the water so that it lands on the bottom covering the pound/50p coin, you win it.

SURVIVAL

This game, described in Unit Four (page 36), emphasises the importance of basic resources for survival.

▽

UNIT SIX

ROCKS AND STONES

AIM

To find out about the various rocks and stones mentioned in the Bible, and explore the nature of building, both materially and spiritually.

LENGTH OF UNIT

Six to twelve sessions.

WHAT WILL WE BE DOING?

Building a 3-dimensional exhibition about the 'living stones' of the Church.

ACTIVITIES

DESIGN

The 3-dimensional exhibition will need to be practical, attractive and informative. It needs to be reasonably portable, so that other churches can borrow it if they wish. Above all it needs to express the basic truth that the Church is built firmly on the foundation of Christ, and in its structure every stone — whether large or small — is important and necessary.

Several heads together are often very productive, so have small groups of three or four people having a go at sketching some designs for the exhibition. All the best ideas could be incorporated in the final structure, with each group being responsible for a section.

PRODUCTION

The compilation of material for the exhibition is run on the lines of newspaper publication, so the group will need to nominate an editor, researchers, illustrators, a photographer and construction workers in order to work most efficiently. This is both a valuable and an enjoyable experience which helps develop the awareness of interdependence and individual value within the group. So the 'living stones' teaching will be going on implicitly as well as explicitly.

RESEARCH

It is important that, although facilitated by the leader, the exhibition should belong to the group and grow out of their own discussion and research. 'Thinking Things Out' will be a starter, and follow-up material is suggested for each session in this unit as resources to be used in research for the exhibition.

Since we are researching a living organism here, the resources will not stop at published books; they will often be people, and sometimes places.

Presentation of material needs to be eye-catching and thought-provoking as well as informative. A single question or statement in bold lettering is often more valuable than a page of tiny writing copied out of a book. Use colour, spacing, maps, coloured tapes, different shapes of mounting paper, different textures and materials to make the researched material digestible to those who will visit the exhibition. You might consider having a taped commentary to assist people, such as is used in many excellent public exhibitions in museums and cathedrals.

VISITS

As a way of inspiring the group with ideas, visit other exhibitions and look critically at their effectiveness. There are often such displays at local libraries and museums, but try to go to one or two of the nationally acclaimed exhibitions as well, such as:

☐ The Oxford Story at Oxford.

☐ The Jorvik exhibition at York.

☐ The Pilgrims' Way at Canterbury.

☐ The London museums.

☐ The Glasgow museums.

☐ The industrial museums at Bristol and Sheffield.

ILLUSTRATION

The idea of the illustration is to provide pictures which help people understand something of the rich and varied life of the church in the area. There should be pictures of communal and individual worship, for instance; pictures of community activities; pictures of different types of ministry and of different age groups involved; pictures of problems which the church is praying for, and pictures of that prayer being put into action.

Encourage the use of a variety of media and methods of expression, such as photography, sketches, paintings, collage, relief work, cartoons etc. Make sure the editors keep a close check on what is being produced so that all areas are illustrated and not just a few, to excess.

▽

Naturally, as work progresses and enthusiasm grows, the pictures will sometimes suggest new lines of research, so the group will need to have frequent progress reports, and recognise the value of flexibility.

CONSTRUCTION

Discuss with the group the kind of materials which would be most suitable for the designs they have made. Cartons and boxes come in a variety of sizes and are fairly lightweight; inner rolls from carpets are strong and versatile; a constructed wooden frame might be covered with paper or card; you may have access to some industrial packaging which could be used. Don't immediately discount anything offered — it may be unusual, but it could be just what is needed!

Be prepared to experiment a bit before the perfect solution is found to a problem; the experimental stages are extremely valuable, even if they end up as a mangled heap of rubbish.

Also bear in mind the value of making the exhibition suitable for dismantling and reconstructing somewhere else. It shouldn't be too fragile, or too heavy.

SESSION ONE

Mountains

THINKING THINGS OUT

Have small groups of three or four people, and give each group a selection of pictures of different mountains and mountain ranges from all over the world. Useful sources are travel brochures and magazines and calendars. Each group will also need an atlas. The task is to see if they can find the pictured mountains in the atlas.

1 In the large group, share what you have found out. A world map for the wall is useful, as you can then stick a coloured pin in each mountain place.

What mountains have been visited by people in the group? They may like to share with the group one thing that impressed them about the mountain they have seen.

To read together: Psalm 125:1-2; Psalm 36:5-6; Psalm 65:6; Psalm 93:1-2.

2 Make a list of words which you could use to describe a mountain. Could some of these qualities apply to God?

3 Why do you think primitive peoples often use mountains as holy places of worship?

4 How do the psalmists use mountains as a symbol?

5 Can you think of any events of Jesus' life which took place in the mountains? If you are struggling, these references will help you: Matthew 4:1-3; Matthew 5:1; Luke 9:28-29; Luke 22:39-42; Matthew 28:16-20; Acts 1:10-12.

6 Why do you think the gospel writers thought it important to mention where these events took place?

WORSHIP

Gather round in a semi-circle and show some slides of mountains, preferably mountains in the Holy Land. These can be borrowed from Christian resource centres, or there may be someone in the parish who has visited the Holy Land and has slides to lend. While the slides are being shown, sing together *Laudate Dominum* (Taizé). Let the singing fade into a time of silence.

Reader 1 Isaiah 54:10; 55:12-13.

'The mountains may be shaken and the hills be eroded to dust, but my love for you will never be shaken, nor my promise of peace be eroded.'

All So says the Lord who loves you with compassion.

Reader 2 'The mountains and the hills will burst into song, and all the trees of the fields will clap their hands.

Where there are brambles the cypress tree will grow;

myrtles will flourish in place of the nettles.'

All So says the Lord who loves you with compassion.

Sing together a song or chorus such as:
Though the mountains may fall (MSOTS)
How lovely on the mountains (HOAN)
At the name of Jesus (HOAN)
Ring out your joy (HOAN)

Reader 1 Father, we thank you

All for the way you love and care for us
every moment of every day of every year.

Reader 1 Father, we ask you

All to make us loyal in our friendships,
trustworthy in our promises,
and reliable in our responsibilities. Amen.

SESSION TWO
Commands

THINKING THINGS OUT

1 In small groups of two or three people, try making up ten basic rules which you think would make for a peaceful, just society.

2 In the large group, swap ideas for the ten rules, writing them up on flipchart or board.

3 Which rules were thought of most often?

4 Which rules are the most important, do you think?

To read together: Exodus 20:1-21.

5 Are these rules, for an ancient, nomadic society, in any way similar to the rules you have designed?

6 Where was Moses when the commandments were given?

7 What does this reading suggest about the relationship between God and the people?

8 Jesus summarised the commandments as 'Love God and love your neighbour'. Which commands would go in each category, do you think?

9 What were the commandments written on? What might this suggest to a nomadic people whose history was handed down by word of mouth?

WORSHIP
Gather round in a circle with a large stone in the centre. Sing *Love is his Word* (HOAN) and let the singing fade into a time of silence.

Reader 1 Jeremiah 31:33-34.
The Lord declares, 'This is the new covenant I will make with the people of Israel when that time has arrived:

Reader 2 I shall plant my law within their minds and write it on their hearts. I shall be their God, and they shall be my people. It will no longer be necessary for anyone to teach their neighbours or their family to know the Lord, because everyone will know me already, from the least important to the most powerful. For I shall forgive their wickedness and never again bring their sin to mind,' declares the Lord.

All Lord, let your will be done in us.

> Sing together a song or chorus such as:
> *A new commandment* (HOAN)
> *We cry 'Hosanna, Lord'* (HOAN)
> *Take me, Lord, use my life* (HOAN)
> *All over the world* (HOAN)
> *Peace, perfect peace* (HOAN)

Reader 1 Father, we thank you

All for your forgiving love
and for your constant encouragement.

Reader 1 Father, we ask you

All to help us live
according to your law of love
wherever we go
and whoever we are with. Amen.

SESSION THREE
Stone-throwing

THINKING THINGS OUT
Following on from the ten rules devised last time, work in the same small groups to devise ways of dealing with those who break the rules of your society.

1 In the large group, swap ideas about punishments or other ways of treating law-breakers and make a note of the main ideas on a board or flipchart, alongside last week's rules.

2 Which of the ideas suggest punishment, which suggest deterrence, and which suggest some kind of healing or re-educating?

3 Do you think that having rules actually tempts you to behave badly, sometimes?

To read together: Leviticus 24:10-17.

4 In a stoning, the whole community took part. Why do you think this was?

5 'A life for a life' is certainly fair. But what are the drawbacks in such a system of punishment? (Think of the Mafia.)

6 Which do you think is more important — justice or mercy?

7 Bearing in mind the society concerned in our reading, do you think stoning was a suitable punishment? Why do you think such harsh punishments were considered necessary?

WORSHIP

Gather round in a circle and in the centre have a group of stones in the shape of a cross, with votive candles set among them. Sing together *Jesus, remember me when you come into your kingdom* (Taizé) and let the singing fade into a time of silence.

Reader 1 Acts 7:57-60.

When they heard what Stephen said, all the members of the Council yelled out at the top of their voice, and covered their ears with their hands. Immediately they all rushed upon Stephen, threw him out of the city and stoned him. And the witnesses left their coats at the feet of a young man called Saul.

Reader 2 And while they were stoning Stephen, he was calling on the Lord, praying, 'Lord Jesus, receive my spirit!' As he fell to his knees he cried out with a loud voice, 'O Lord, do not hold this sin against them!' And having said this, he died.

All Father, forgive us
for the cruelty and torture
of our world.
Give us courage to stand firm
and fight against evil,
even at the expense
of our own safety.

Sing together a song or chorus such as:
Do not be afraid (HOAN)
If God is for us (SOTS)
Be bold, be strong (SOF4)
God forgave my sin (HOAN)

Reader 1 Father, we thank you
All for the work of all who struggle against oppression and injustice.
Reader 1 Father, we ask you
All to encourage and support
all those who are suffering pain
or imprisonment
because of their faith. Amen.

SESSION FOUR

The temple

THINKING THINGS OUT

1 In small groups of three or four, try drawing a plan of Solomon's temple from the description in 1 Kings 6.

2 In the large group, have a look at all the plans and enjoy them. Look at an artist's impression of the temple (many Bible commentaries have clear ones) to get an even better idea of its size and magnificence.

3 What was placed in the holy of holies in the temple, do you think? (Cast your mind back a couple of sessions, or look at 1 Kings 6:19-22; 2 Chronicles 5:10.)

4 What do you think the temple was for? It may help to read 1 Kings 6:11-13.

5 Have a look at the number of craftsmen involved. (1 Kings 5:13-18; 2 Chronicles 2:17-18) What do you think this tells us about Solomon and the people of Israel?

6 Look at 2 Chronicles 4:1-6. What does this tell you about the worship? Can you imagine what it would have looked/sounded/smelt like?

7 If you had been one of those involved, how do you think you would have felt when the temple was finally complete?

To read together: John 2:13-17.

8 Knowing the enthusiasm and care that had gone into the making of Solomon's temple, can you see why Jesus was so angry about the way the temple was being used in his day?

9 Sometimes Jesus talked of himself as being God's temple. In the light of what you now know about the temple, what do you think he meant?

WORSHIP

Gather round in a circle, with an arrangement of candles and flowers in the centre. Sing together *Our hearts were made for you, Lord* (HOAN) and let the singing fade into a time of silence.

Reader 1 John 4:19-24.

The woman says to Jesus, 'O sir, I can see that you are a prophet. Our fathers worshipped on this mountain, but you Jews say that Jerusalem is the place where people ought to worship God.'

Reader 2 Jesus says to the woman, 'Woman, believe me, that a time is coming when you will worship the Father neither on this mountain, nor in Jerusalem. You Samaritans worship what you do not know; we worship what we know, because salvation comes from the Jews. But a time is coming — and is already here — when the true worshippers will worship the Father in spirit and truth: that is the kind of worshipper the Father wants to find. God is Spirit, so people can only truly worship him in spirit and in truth.'

All Psalm 51:16-17.
You do not take delight in sacrifices, or I would offer one;
you do not want burnt offerings.
The sacrifice you require of me is a humble spirit, O God;
a broken and repentant heart you will never despise.

Sing together a hymn or chorus such as:
 Here I am, Lord (SOTS3)
 When the Spirit of the Lord (SOF)
 Earthen vessels (SOTS3)

Reader 1 Father, we thank you

All for the freedom to worship you openly.

Reader 2 Father, we ask you

All to encourage and support all those for whom worship brings danger and persecution. Amen.

SESSION FIVE

Strong foundations

THINKING THINGS OUT

In small groups of three or four, try building a house of cards, with each member of the group taking turns to add a card. For best results, try not to breathe!

1 If possible, view one another's masterpieces before they collapse. Then come into a large group. What were some of the construction problems that you faced during the building?

2 Which cards did you find were the most important to place exactly right?

3 Would the foundation you were working on affect the strength of your house?

To read together: Luke 6:46-49.

4 What would have been the advantages of building on sand? (Might it be quicker? Easier? Cheaper?)

5 When the houses were first built, would one have looked any weaker than the other?

6 Think now of your own life as a house. In what ways can we build our lives on sand or rock?

7 What might we feel are the advantages of building on 'sand'?

8 Still thinking of the story as a picture of life, what do you think the floods and storms are?

9 Can you think of any times you have witnessed a 'house' stand firm throughout 'storms' — either in your own life or in the life of someone else?

WORSHIP

Gather round in a circle with some building materials in the centre. Sing together *Build, build*

your Church (HOAN) and let the singing fade into a time of silence.

Reader 1 Psalm 127:1.
 Unless the Lord builds the house,

All the work of the builders is useless.

Reader 1 Unless the Lord is protecting the city,

All the sentries stand guard in vain.

Reader 2 Jeremiah 17:7-8.
 Blessed is anyone who trusts in the Lord and relies on him.
 Such a person is like a tree growing close beside the water
 with its roots stretching out towards the stream.
 When hot weather comes it is not afraid,
 and its leaves stay green.
 In years of drought it is not worried,
 and carries on yielding fruit.

Sing together a hymn or chorus such as:
 I am a new creation (SOF)
 How great is our God (HOAN)
 Oh the love of my Lord (HOAN)
 Our hearts were made for you (HOAN)

Reader 1 Father, we thank you,

All for you are our strong rock
 and we know we can always trust you.

Reader 1 Father, we ask you

All to help and strengthen
 all those who feel lost, rejected or bewildered;
 and strengthen our faith
 so we can serve you better. Amen.

47

SESSION SIX
Living stones

THINKING THINGS OUT

1 On the resource sheet for this session is an outline of a church built with stones. In small groups of two or three, fill in the stones with the names of all the different activities and ministries of the parish you can think of.

2 In the large group, share and compare one another's view of the parish. Are there any areas of need which are not being cared for? What are they?

3 Obviously stones are a strong building material. What else do we need, apart from lots of stones, to make a safe, attractive and strong building? (Architect? Good builders? Cement? No big gaps?)

4 How is this like the living 'stones' of the Church?

5 In the living Church, what might be the cement that binds us together?

To read together: Ephesians 2:18-22.

6 That was Paul's answer to question 4! Do you think it is true of the Church today?

7 How was the early Church different from today, and how was it very similar? You will need to look at Acts 2:42-47 to answer this question.

8 Many people outside the Church only think of it as a building. How can we make sure we really are 'a place where God lives through his Spirit'?

WORSHIP

Gather round in a circle with a circle of candles burning in the centre. Sing together *Peace, perfect peace* (HOAN) and let the singing fade into a time of silence.

Reader 1 Acts 4:31-35.
> And when they had finished praying, the building where they were gathered was shaken, and they were all filled with the Holy Spirit, and proclaimed the word of God fearlessly.

Reader 2 The whole company of believers was united in heart and soul. No one claimed any possessions as their own, but all their resources were pooled.

Reader 1 And with great power the apostles testified to the resurrection of the Lord Jesus; rich blessings were poured out on them all. No one among them was ever left in need, because those who owned land or houses were selling their property, bringing money from the sale and presenting it to the apostles. The money was distributed to everyone according to their needs.

Sing together a hymn or chorus such as:
Majesty, worship his majesty (HOAN)
Father God I wonder (SOF)
Ring out your joy (HOAN)
Lord Jesus Christ (HOAN)

Reader 1 Father, we thank you

All for coming to us
and filling us with joy and peace.

Reader 1 Father, we ask you

All to fill us all to overflowing
with your living Spirit,
for you are our God, and we worship you!
Amen.

GAMES

STEPPING STONES
Stepping stones cut out of newspapers are scattered around the floor and everyone moves around freely. At the shout of 'Alligators!' everyone rushes to find a space on a safe stepping stone. Each time one stepping stone is removed, until everyone is squashed on to the same stone. If you can't squeeze on to a stone you're out. The winners are those who manage to find a place on the final stone.

BUILD A TOWER
Divide into teams of six people and make an obstacle route from one end of the room to the other. Have six cartons (the larger the better) at one end of the room. You will also need a stopwatch. Each team member in turn picks up a 'stone' and carries it through and over the obstacles to build a six-storey tower at the other end. Each team's effort is timed and the fastest team wins. If you have enough cartons and obstacles you could have all the teams building at the same time, but part of the fun is enjoying watching the others!

CHURCH DRIVE

This is a beetle drive with a church building to be constructed rather than a beetle. Show this picture so everyone knows what to draw.

The cost of each unit is as follows:

Foundation stone	6	(This must be thrown before everything else)
Door	5	
Window	4	
Spire	3	
Clock	2	
Stones	1	

BALLOON PYRAMIDS

Divide into groups of three or four for this. The task is to build a metre-high pyramid out of balloons and shaving cream. It is advisable to play this outside!

SEA WALL

If you live near the coast, try a sea wall building competition when the tide is coming in. Ask everyone to bring a spade of some kind and whichever team's sea wall withstands the tide longest wins. If weather conditions are reasonable, you could combine this with a beach barbecue, and have the whole session on the beach, including 'Thinking Things Out' and Worship.

DAMS

For those living near streams or rivers, dam building is an alternative to sea wall building. Make sure that any stream played with in this way is returned to its original state before you leave it.

FORFEITS

Linked with the theme of laws and punishments, this traditional game is still good fun, so long as the forfeits are not in any way cruel or over-embarrassing. Spinning a tray for a named person to pick up before it falls is the usual way of starting, but you could vary this if the group has another idea. Those failing to catch the tray are given a forfeit to do. Let the group devise the forfeits themselves before you play the game.

SCAVENGER HUNT

Following the idea of collecting materials for a special building, send people out to collect a list of items which sound like building materials: gold, silver, wood, stone, brick, glass, metal, clay etc. They try to make their collection take up as little space as possible — a matchbox, for example.

UNIT SEVEN

WATER

AIM

To explore the value of water, both physically and spiritually.

LENGTH OF UNIT

Six to twelve sessions.

WHAT WILL WE BE DOING?

Providing a fresh water supply for a village in a developing country.

ACTIVITIES

FACT FINDING

Many charities have excellent education programmes and are willing to come and spend time with groups to inform and encourage a deeper awareness of what the needs are. Here are some useful addresses:

CAFOD, 2 Romero Close, Stockwell Road, London SW9 9TY.
ACTION AID, Hamlyn House, Archway, London N19 5PG.
CHRISTIAN AID, PO Box 100, London SE1 7RT.
OXFAM, 274 Banbury Road, Oxford OX2 7DZ.

The charities have a considerable amount of material to use as a resource for further research. You can also use the local library and Christian resource centre, and members of the group can write to other organisations and people working in developing countries. The aim is to make the whole group more aware and alive to the pressing need for water supplies and health facilities, so that they are spurred on to help in a practical way.

ADOPTION

After the group has found out the different needs, the next stage is to decide where the water supply will be. Often the best idea is to adopt a particular village; the link is then very personal and people feel more immediately involved. Again, the charities will supply the necessary information, but do supplement this by encouraging research into the exact location, the climate, the clothes and homes, the art and craft, the music, family life etc. so that a full interest can be taken and the project can be seen to be a two-way exchange of friendships, rather than a one-sided gift.

FUND RAISING

This needs to be done in ways which are appropriate to the project and will capture the imagination of those asked to contribute. If you discuss this with the group after their fact-finding, the ideas will probably come thick and fast, but here are a few suggestions to get you going:

2 A sponsored water carry from the town centre to a local church.

2 Water selling. Sell water in paper cups for as much money as people are prepared to give. Warm days in shopping centres or on sea fronts are a good idea for this one.

3 A sponsored swim: 'through the water for the water'.

4 A sponsored walk. Walk backwards and forwards along the distance it is for people in your adopted village to reach their water supply. To make this more vivid to passers-by, build a hut out of carpet, inner tubes and branches at one end of the walk, and have a paddling pool of muddy water at the other end.

WELL-DIGGING

First choose a site where digging wells is definitely allowed! Then dig down until you find water. Measure the depth and then devise an efficient method of hauling the water up to the surface. If you feel inclined to sample it, make sure you boil it thoroughly first!

SESSION ONE

Water! Water!

THINKING THINGS OUT

Ask everyone to guess how much water is used in a day by the whole group. When they have written their guess down, collect in the named slips. Now give out the resource sheet and ask everyone to complete the chart about how much water they have used.

1 In the large group, compare results, and on a flipchart write the combined totals for the whole group. Was the amount different from what you expected? Which guess was nearest the truth?

2 Where does all our water come from?

3 Have a look at a world rainfall map. Where are the driest and wettest areas of our world? Do they coincide with areas of need?

4 How can we save water?

To read together: Genesis 1:1-2, 6-10.

5 Many primitive people thought water was the first created substance. Pretend that you have no scientific knowledge at all. Now, from the facts you have gained from experience, why do you think they thought this?

6 In what ways are we damaging this essential ingredient of life?

WORSHIP

Gather round in a circle with a bowl of water in the centre and a lighted floating candle on it. Sing together *Lord the light of your love is shining* (SOF4) and let the singing fade into a time of silence.

Reader 1 Exodus 15:22-27.

Moses led the people of Israel away from the Sea of Reeds into the desert of Shur, and they travelled for three days without finding water.

When they reached Marah the water there was so bitter that they could not drink it. (That is why the place is called Marah, which means 'bitter' in Hebrew.) So the people complained to Moses, saying,

All 'What are we to drink?'

Reader 2 Moses poured out his heart to the Lord, and the Lord showed him a piece of wood. When he threw it into the water, the water became sweet enough to drink ... So eventually they came to Elim, where there were twelve springs and seventy palm trees, and there by the water they pitched their camp.

Sing together a hymn or chorus such as:
Peace is flowing like a river (HOAN)
As the deer pants (SOF)
Make me a channel of your peace (HOAN)
The cry of the poor (SOTS3)
Listen! (HOAN)

Reader 1 As a deer longs for a stream of cool water,

All so I long for you, O God.
I thirst for you, the living God.

Reader 2 Lord, you are the fountain of love;

All fill us all to overflowing
and bless all those who live in the village of (name). Amen.

SESSION TWO

Flood

THINKING THINGS OUT

First divide into twos and swap memories of floods seen on the news or experienced at home or elsewhere. How deep was the water? What did it look like? What were people wearing? What happened to cars? Possessions? Crops? Soil?

1 In the large group come together and share some of the stories. Do you think floods are entirely destructive, or can they have some good effects? If so, what?

To read together: Genesis 6:5-22.

2 Why did God want to destroy the world which he had created out of love?

3 Have you ever felt let down by someone or something you had high hopes of?

4 Perhaps those who have could share with the others how they felt.

5 Imagine you are one of those in the ark. How do you feel as the flood waters destroy all other life?

6 Now imagine you are stepping out on to the muddy ground. How do you feel about the future?

7 How do you think God might feel about the future?

8 Do you ever think we deserve to be destroyed?

9 Has it ever occurred to you that the God who created us has the power to destroy us if he so chooses?

10 The rainbow was a sign of God's promise. What was the promise? (Genesis 9:12-17).

▽

WORSHIP

Gather round in a circle with a rainbow in the centre, made with a bowl of water, a mirror and a light, like this:

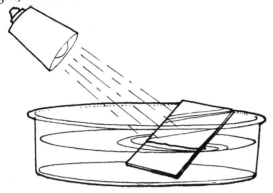

Sing together *Rise and shine and give God the glory* (Alleluya!) and after the singing have a time of silence.

Reader 1 Matthew 24:37-42.

As it was at the time of Noah, so it will be when the Son of Man comes. For in the days before the flood, people were eating and drinking, marrying and being given in marriage, right up to the day when Noah went into the ark. And no one understood the significance of what was happening until the flood came and swept them all away.

Reader 2 It will be just like that when the Son of Man comes. Then, two men will be working in the fields — one will be taken, the other left behind. Two women will be grinding corn at a mill — one will be taken, the other left behind.

All Be watchful, then, because you do not know which day your Lord will come.

Sing together a hymn or chorus such as:
Send forth your Spirit (HOAN)
Do not be afraid (HOAN)
You shall cross the barren desert (MSOTS)
Lord, when I turn my back on you (HOAN)

Reader 1 I depend on God alone,

All I put my hope in him.

Reader 2 Lord, protect and save us,

All for you are our strong rock and our shelter. Amen.

SESSION THREE

Wells

THINKING THINGS OUT

Give out the resource sheet with the quiz on wells. They can work in small groups and each group will need a Bible.

[1] In the large group discuss what you have found out. Why do you think wells are mentioned often in the Bible? Bear in mind the climate and terrain of the Holy Land. It might be helpful to see some pictures.

[2] Imagine you are collecting water for your family and notice the well is nearly dry. What worries and plans go through your mind?

To read together: Genesis 24:11-20.

[3] Why do you think the servant thought this was a good way of choosing a suitable wife for Isaac?

[4] What good qualities did Rebecca show?

[5] Compare her reaction with that of the Samaritan woman whom Jesus asked for a drink (John 4:7-9).

[6] Jesus referred to himself as a well. Now that you know something of the importance of wells in their society, what do you think he meant?

[7] Have you ever been really thirsty? If so, tell the others what it was like.

[8] Have you ever felt this 'thirsty' for meaning in life or for some particular ambition?

WORSHIP

Gather round in a circle with a stone jar or a bucket of water in the centre, surrounded by stones and sand on a groundsheet. Sing together *Oh come to the water* (HOAN) and let the singing fade into a time of silence.

Reader 1 John 4:10-15.

Jesus answered the woman, 'If you only knew the gift God gives, and who it is asking you for a drink, it would be you asking him for a drink, and he would give you living water.'

Reader 2 'Oh Sir,' said the woman, 'you have nothing to draw the water up with, and the well is deep. So where have you got this living water from?'

Reader 1 In answer to her, Jesus replied, 'Anyone drinking this water will get thirsty again, but whoever drinks of the water I shall give him need never be thirsty again. But the water I shall give you will become in you a spring welling up for eternity.'

Reader 2 The woman said to him, 'Sir, give me this water!'

Sing together a hymn or chorus such as:
Breathe on me breath of God (HOAN)
I waited patiently (SOF)
Lord give me also springs of water (SOF)
O Lord, your tenderness (SOF 4)

Reader 1 The Lord is my shepherd;

All there is nothing more I need.

Reader 1 He gives me rest in green meadows of grass,

All and leads me to calm pools of fresh water.

Reader 2 Father, we bring to your living water

All all who thirst for fresh drinking water
and all who thirst for peace, goodness and justice. Amen.

SESSION FOUR
Washing

THINKING THINGS OUT
Give out the resource sheet and let everyone have a go at the Naaman quiz. They can work in small groups and will need a Bible for each group.

1 In the large group discuss what you have found out. If you had been Naaman, do you think you would have done what Elisha advised straight away, or after persuasion or not at all?

2 Why was Naaman annoyed about what he was told to do?

3 When is water used to soothe and help healing today?

4 Washing became an important ritual for the people of Israel, particularly in connection with eating, washing a traveller's feet etc. Remembering what you know of their climate and lifestyle, why do you think this ritual washing was so important to them?

To read together: Luke 7:36-39; 44-47.

5 Imagine you are one of Simon's guests. How do you feel when the woman starts washing Jesus' feet with her tears?

6 Bearing in mind what we know of the social good manners of the time, what does this episode tell us about Simon? About the woman? About Jesus?

7 Foot-washing was usually the lowest servant's job. Imagine you are one of the disciples at the Last Supper. How do you feel as Jesus bends down to wash your feet?

8 How can we 'wash one another's feet'?

WORSHIP
Gather round in a circle with a jar of water, a bowl and a towel in the centre. Sing together *River wash over me* (SOF) and let the singing fade into a time of silence.

Reader 1 Psalm 51:1-2, 12.
O God, in your kindness have mercy on me and in your compassion blot out my offence! Wash me and wash me from all of my guilt and cleanse me from all of my sin . . . Restore to me the joy that comes from your salvation.

Reader 2 Ezekiel 36:24-29.
I shall take you out from among the nations, gather you up from every country, and bring you back to your own land. I shall sprinkle clean water over you and you will be cleansed; I shall wash you clean of all your idols and of all that has defiled you. I shall give you a new heart and put a new spirit in you . . . I shall save you from all that defiles you.

Sing together a hymn or chorus such as:
O God my creator (SOF)
Mud on my eyes (Garth Hewitt)
Take me Lord (HOAN)
Our hearts were made for you (HOAN)

Reader 3 Like a dry, worn-out and waterless land,

All my soul is thirsty for you.

Reader 3 Your constant love is better than life itself,

All and so I will praise you.

Reader 3 My soul will feast and be satisfied,

All and I will sing glad songs of praise to you.

Reader 4 Lord Jesus, as you washed your disciples' feet,

All help us delight in washing one another's feet in love. Amen.

SESSION FIVE
Stormy water

THINKING THINGS OUT

In small groups of three or four people, collect five facts about the sea of Galilee and write them on the resource sheets. Each group will need an atlas or a map of the area and an information/travel book about the area. These can be borrowed from libraries and Christian resource centres, or you may have a church library.

1 Galilee is notorious for violent storms that suddenly blow up and endanger boats. Can you think of a time when this happened to Jesus and his disciples?

To read together: Matthew 8:23-27.

2 Why do you think Jesus was able to sleep through the storm? (There may be several different reasons.)

3 Imagine you are in the boat, bailing out water as fast as you can. You look across and see Jesus still asleep. How do you feel?

4 When the disciples were wondering 'what kind of man is this?' what thoughts might have gone through their minds? You might like to look at these references: Genesis 1:2; 1 Kings 19:12; Exodus 14:21; Psalm 57:1.

5 We sometimes talk of finding life 'stormy'. On the chart, list some of the characteristics of weather storms in one column, and in another column match them with some of the characteristics of life storms.

6 Have you ever been given peace in the middle of a bad patch in your life? If so, you may like to help the group by explaining how you felt. (Or read 'Footprints'.)

WORSHIP

Gather round in a circle with a lighted floating candle on a bowl of water in the centre. Sing together *Dear Lord and Father of mankind* (HOAN) and let the singing fade into a time of silence.

Reader 1 Luke 8:27-35.
> As Jesus was stepping ashore he was met by a man from the town who was possessed by demons. For a long time this man had not worn any clothes, and he would not stay in a house, but lived out among the burial caves.

Reader 2 As soon as he saw Jesus he started crying out and threw himself down at Jesus' feet, screaming,

All 'What do you want with me, Jesus, Son of the Most High God? I beg you, don't torment me!'

Reader 1 And Jesus asked him,

Reader 2 'What is your name?'

All 'My name is "Many",' he answered,

Reader 1 because many demons had entered him. When the people from the local town and villages came to see what had been going on, they found the man from whom the demons had gone out, sitting at the feet of Jesus, dressed and perfectly sane.

FOOTPRINTS IN THE SAND
One night I had a dream.
I was walking along the beach with the Lord,
and across the skies flashed scenes from my life.
In each scene I noticed two sets of footprints
   in the sand.
One was mine, and one was the Lord's.
When the last scene of my life appeared before me,
I looked back at the footprints in the sand,
and, to my surprise, I noticed that many times
along the path of my life there was only one set
   of footprints.
And I noticed that it was at the lowest and saddest
   times in my life.
I asked the Lord about it.
'Jesus, you said that once I decided to follow you,
you would walk with me all the way.
But I notice that during the most troublesome
   times in my life
there was only one set of footprints.
I don't understand why you left my side
when I needed you most.'
The Lord said, 'My precious child,
I never left you during your time of trial.
Where you see only one set of footprints,
I was carrying you.'

Sing together a hymn or chorus such as:
Walk with me, O my Lord (HOAN)
Do not be afraid (HOAN)
Give thanks (SOF4)
Peace, perfect peace (HOAN)

Reader 3 Lord God Almighty,
  none is as mighty as you;

All in all things you are faithful, O Lord.

Reader 3 You rule over the powerful sea;

All you calm its angry waves.

Reader 4 Father, when our life feels like a raging sea

All give us the reassurance of your peace. Amen.

SESSION SIX

Water of new life

THINKING THINGS OUT

First give everyone the John the Baptist quiz on the resource sheet to try. They can work in small groups, and each group will need a Bible.

1 In the large group discuss what you have found out about John the Baptist, and enjoy one another's identikit pictures of him. If you had been one of the crowd by the river Jordan, would you have gone to be baptised, do you think?

2 What strikes you most about John's teaching — a love for people, the practical advice, the challenge, or what?

3 In the Jordan the people were completely submerged during baptism. What do you think this would symbolise? (Think back to Noah, and to the Red Sea crossing.)

4 What is symbolised by the person emerging alive from the water in baptism?

To read together: Matthew 3:13-15.

5 Why didn't John want to baptise Jesus?

6 Why do you think Jesus felt it right that he should be baptised, even though he had no need of cleansing from sin?

7 Have a look at Acts 2:37-41. The people are advised not just to be baptised, but to be baptised 'in the name of the Lord Jesus'. What is the difference?

8 What did Peter tell the people they would get if they did so?

9 Is there a danger that in making baptism freely available, we lose sight of the life-changing commitment that is being made?

WORSHIP

Gather round in a circle either in a room, with a bowl of water surrounded by flowers and candles in the centre, or outside near some water, such as a pond, stream, lake or the sea. Sing together *Veni Sancti Spiritus* (Taizé) and let the singing fade into a time of silence.

Reader 1 Exodus 14:21-22.
  Then Moses stretched out his hand over the sea, and all through that night the Lord drove the sea back with a strong east wind, turning the sea into dry land. The water was divided and the Israelites walked on dry ground right through the sea, with walls of water on either side of them.

Reader 2 Matthew 28:16-20.
  Then the eleven disciples went to the mountain in Galilee where Jesus had told them to go . . . Jesus came up to them and spoke to them.

Reader 3 'All authority in heaven and earth has been given to me. Go, then, make disciples of all nations, baptising them into the name of the Father, and of the Son, and of the Holy Spirit. Teach them to keep all the commands I have given you. And know this: I shall be with you always, to the very end of time.'

> Sing together a hymn or chorus such as:
> *How great is our God* (HOAN)
> *I am a new creation* (SOF)
> *Spirit of the living God* (HOAN)
> *Spirit of God please fill me now* (SOF)

Reader 3 You welcome me as an honoured guest

All and fill my cup to the brim.

Reader 3 I know that your goodness and love
  will be with me all my life;

All and your house will be my home as long as I live. Amen.

GAMES

SWIMMING GAMES

An obvious choice! A visit to the local pool or beach is always popular, and games like playing around in the water and racing really organise themselves. Other possibilities are:

- [ ] 'Shark' which is a water version of catch. The shark can only catch people in the water, but you can't stay out of the water for more than the time it takes to spell S.H.A.R.K. Depending on the skill of your swimmers, you could make this an entirely underwater game, though you are allowed up for breathers sometimes!

- [ ] Water polo where you score by touching the ball on to the walkway at either end of the pool.

- [ ] Whales. Groups dive down and hang under the water, singing whale songs to one another. The sound effects are really strange.

- [ ] River crossing. The idea is to swim across the pool with various items such as clothing or a mug, without getting them wet at all.

- [ ] Diving for pennies, or for golf balls or anything safe and sinkable.

WATER SLIDING

This is definitely one for warm weather. Spread dustbin bags out in a long continuous line and hose them down freely for a tremendous (and cheap) water slide. If you plan to use this often it's worth stitching the bags together. If not, sellotape on the underside works temporarily.

WHOSE HOSE?

One person starts with the hose and the others are some distance all around. They try to creep up and reach the hoser without being hosed. If they succeed, they have the next turn with the hose.

BEACH COMBING

Set out to find particular things, or just go and see what you can find.

POND DIPPING

Stress the need for suitable clothes, take a few reference books, containers and nets and enjoy!

UNIT EIGHT

FOOD

AIM

To explore the ways we are fed, both physically and spiritually, and the ways we feed one another.

LENGTH OF UNIT

Six to twelve sessions.

WHAT WILL WE BE DOING?

Compiling a parish recipe book and making a Communion set of chalice, ciborium, candle holders, and altar frontal.

ACTIVITIES

CLAY

Ask at local craft shops for information leading you to a good supplier of clay; this is far less expensive if bought in bulk, and you may well find people willing to give a discount for a voluntary parish group.

Before anything else, protect all surfaces and floors and have bowls of water available for rinsing hands, as clay has the unfortunate habit of clogging sinks.

Allow time for everyone to enjoy the feel of the material before going on to experimenting with different designs for candle holders. It is a good idea to have some stumps of the church candles available for getting the size right. The clay holder should be slightly larger than necessary at the moment so as to allow for shrinkage as it dries out.

The Communion set could be achieved with slab work, a glorified thumb pot, or using the coiling technique. Any unfinished masterpieces will need to be wrapped in damp paper and polythene to keep them in workable condition for the following session. Collect an assortment of nails, sticks, old sieves, tooth picks etc. to use in patterning the clay before leaving it to dry slowly and thoroughly before firing.

Schools, colleges, amateur potters or craft shops are all possibilities when it comes to sharing the use of a kiln. After firing, the pots can be glazed and fired. Make sure that the pieces are very smooth underneath as well as on top, and that any coils are thoroughly smoothed together, before firing, so as to avoid disasters.

COOKING

This is always popular! Over the weeks available try a variety of ingredients and cooking methods, using both conventional ovens and also open fire cooking and improvised ovens, and the American Indian method of placing hot clean(!) stones into a container. The Indians used buffalo hides, but metal pots are just as good.

Try stone-grinding barley or wheat into flour (N.B. Don't use stone that erodes easily — it's bad for the teeth!), roasting meat on wooden skewers, barbecuing fish, cooking potatoes at the bottom of a fire, toasting banana and marshmallow kebabs, preparing raw vegetables for a cheese fondue, or concocting new and original yoghurt flavours. In other words, be imaginative and inventive; after all, this isn't so much a cookery course as a celebration of the way people all over the world keep themselves alive as pleasantly as possible from the ingredients available to them.

Or you could supply each small group with the same set of ingredients, and see what different results they come up with. It may be worth warning them that they will have to eat what they produce.

Another idea is to have each group bringing and preparing a dish from a different continent or country or age. Local libraries, particularly the children's sections, are useful here. Each group could dress up to match the type of food being prepared. Interested parents of different ethnic groups may be willing to share their expertise and demonstrate cooking a particular favourite food.

BREAD MAKING

Try several different recipes and different flours, so as to compare and contrast them. Experiment with the earliest known form of bread — simply a flour and water dough baked over an open fire. Make some leavened and some unleavened bread and notice the action of the yeast. Collect a variety of breads from the supermarket and have a tasting session; this may include pitta bread, pumpernickel, baguettes etc.

▽

For the celebration of the Eucharist or Agape meal at the end of this unit, the following recipe is useful as it makes a soft bread which is not too crumbly.

Ingredients

1lb of wholemeal flour   ¼pt milk
pinch of salt   2oz butter

1 Mix flour and salt together, and make a well in the centre.

2 Warm the milk and butter to blood heat, and gradually add to the flour.

3 Knead well for 2 minutes.

4 Divide the dough into 24 pieces and flatten each piece to a circle, about ¼ inch thick.

5 Cook each one in a frying pan over a gentle heat until speckled brown.

6 Wrap in a clean cloth until needed.

EMBROIDERY/APPLIQUÉ

The idea is to design and complete an altar frontal and/or chasuble to be worn at the celebration Eucharist at the end of this unit. Although time is limited, don't be tempted to rush the design stage, as in many ways this is the most important part, and the rest of the work will fall into place far more easily if all those involved have a really clear idea of what effect they are working for. Go for simplicity rather than risking a look of fussiness; decide as a group what message you want to convey, what kind of mood you want to express, and then choose shapes and colours to reflect these ideas. Main pieces can be embroidered first and then attached. If you are using a sewing machine, try out various ideas on samples first; these trial runs, together with the designs, can be kept and displayed for the rest of the parish to see in an exhibition of the unit. After all, the preparation is just as important as the finished product, and it can be both enlightening and enriching for people to see the gradual development of the work.

Have charts and books available which show examples of possible stitches, and a wide variety of fabrics, cords, braids, threads etc. Once again, make full use of any skilled people in the parish, encouraging them to work with the group for a session or for the unit.

COMPILING A PARISH RECIPE BOOK

This kind of book always goes down well at fairs and bazaars, and also helps to encourage all-age co-operation in an area which interests *everyone*! Obviously the first task is to collect people's favourite recipes. This may involve writing a short piece for the weekly/monthly bulletin; having a few people to look in on other groups meeting during the week; or collaring people after Sunday and weekday services.

At the same time as collecting recipes, collect names and any interesting snippets of stories and memories prompting the choice of food. All these details will add interest to the book, and will make it very special to the parish. Perhaps a particular cake was baked on a day when some good news came; or perhaps fried onions always conjure up a particularly funny or happy memory. Ask for favourite foods from young children, teenagers, middle-aged people and senior citizens, so that the book is truly representative of all the parish. Include some odd, crazy ones as well, some traditional, some unusual and some completely original. Include recipes for drinks too. It will be quite a book!

Design a cover and do some drawings to go in with the recipes, and finally 'print' the books using a photocopier. Some fund raising, perhaps linked with the cooking activities, may be necessary for initial outlay before you are reimbursed by the sale of copies of the book.

SESSION ONE
Supply and demand

THINKING THINGS OUT

Have a selection of labels from canned and bottled food, together with a number of atlases, or world maps. Give a selection of labels and a world map to each small group. Their task is to find out where all the food comes from and write the answers on the resource sheets. Then bring everyone together. Keep the labels for the next session.

1 What different countries have provided us with this food?

2 Which country provides most variety in our small survey?

3 Do you think we eat what we choose, or do the large firms really decide for us in the way they prepare and package the food?

4 Why do we eat? And how do we know when we are hungry?

To read together: Matthew 4:2-4.

5 How is God's word a kind of bread for us?

6 When would these words 'feed' you: 'Do not be afraid; I shall remain with you always'?

7 And these: 'Come to me all you who are heavily burdened and I will refresh you'?

WORSHIP

Gather round in a circle with a jug of water and a bread roll placed in the centre with a candle. Sing together: *I am the bread of life* (HOAN) and let the singing fade into a time of quietness.

Reader 1 1 Kings 19:3-6.
> Elijah was terrified and fled for his life . . . After walking a day's journey into the desert he sat down under a bushy tree and wished he could die.

Reader 2 'Lord, I can't take any more,' he prayed. 'Take my life — I'm no better than my ancestors.'

Reader 1 Then he lay down under the tree and fell asleep. All at once an angel touched him and said,

Reader 3 'Get up and eat!'

Reader 1 He looked around, and there by his head was a scone baked on hot stones, and a jar of water. He ate and drank and then lay down again.

All Thank you, Father,
for strengthening us and refreshing us,
both with food
and with your loving kindness.

Sing together a song or chorus of thanks and praise, such as:
I will enter his gates (HOAN)
Therefore the redeemed (SOTS3)
Hosanna! hosanna! (SOF4)
Father, we love you (HOAN)

Reader 1 Father, we pray for all who are hungry, all who are starved of food, of friendship, of encouragement, of peace.

Silence

All Lord, feed us with the bread of life. Amen.

PROTEINS

CEREALS

DAIRY PRODUCTS

FRUIT, VEGETABLES

SESSION TWO
Nourishment

THINKING THINGS OUT
Prepare a chart which shows the main food groups like this:

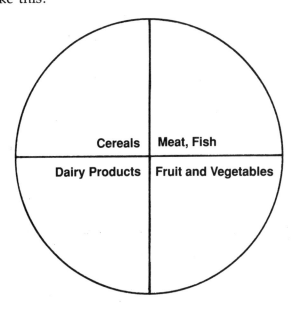

Cereals | Meat, Fish

Dairy Products | Fruit and Vegetables

Have the labels from the last session available again, and in small groups of three or four sort the foods into the different food groups, making notes on the resource sheets. Come together to share the results and write these up on the food chart.

1 What does food do when it nourishes us? (such tasks as building cells, repairing and replacing cells, keeping the body functioning well.)

2 Why do you think 'junk food' is so called?

3 What do you think is spiritual 'junk food'? (such things as reading the stars, ouija boards, materialism — 'if it doesn't make money it must be worthless' etc.)

To read together: John 6:32-35.

4 How can we get complete spiritual nourishment?

5 Have a go at designing a spiritual food chart. (Have another chart with the food groups labelled according to the group's suggestions, but along the lines of: joy, thankfulness, comfort, peace, conscience-jogging, challenge, strength and confidence.)

6 Where would you place these references? Genesis 1:31; Psalm 147:3; Exodus 4:12; Matthew 18:34-35; John 20:19; Ephesians 4:1-2.

WORSHIP

Gather round in a circle, with a tray of bread, cheese, fruit and vegetables on it. If these are already sliced they can be offered round from one person to the next at the end of the worship. Sing together *Farmer, farmer* (MWTP), which is about us being made into God's bread so that the world will be fed. Let the singing fade into a time of silence.

Reader 1 Exodus 16:2, 13-16, 31.

In the desert the whole community began complaining to Moses and Aaron that they had no food ... That evening, a flock of quails flew in, covering the camp; and in the morning there was a layer of dew on the ground surrounding the camp. When the dew had lifted, it left thin flakes like frost on the ground. As soon as the Israelites saw it, they said to one another,

All 'What is it?'

Reader 1 because they no idea what it could be. Moses said to them,

Reader 2 'That is the food which God has provided for you to eat. Now these are the Lord's orders: each one of you is to gather as much of it as you need.'

Reader 1 The people called the food 'manna' (which means 'what is it?'). It was white like coriander seed — and it tasted like wafer biscuits made with honey.

All Father, you nourish us
with food and love
and we thank you.

Sing together a chorus or song such as:
The King of love my shepherd is (HOAN)
Though the mountains may fall (MSOTS)
I will be with you (HOAN)
Oh! How good is the Lord (HOAN)

Reader 2 Father, we pray
for all whose harvests have failed,
for all who are poorly nourished
both physically and spiritually;

All Lord, we are one body, one bread;
remake us and use us
so that the world may be fed. Amen.

SESSION THREE

Feasting

THINKING THINGS OUT

In small groups of three or four, make up a menu for a seven course meal and write them on the resource sheets. Give each group a different guest of honour, so that the menus are varied. Possible 'guests' could be: a member of the Royal Family, the Prime Minister, a famous sports personality, the vicar, the local crossing warden, a television personality.

1 In the large group share the menus and vote on which is the most delicious/unusual/appropriate.

2 Why do people have feasts when a thick sandwich would probably satisfy hunger? (List the reasons on a wall chart.)

To read together: Luke 5:27-29; John 2:1-2; Luke 7:36; Luke 19:2-7.

3 Why did the Pharisees object to the fact that Jesus often went to feasts? (If you are stuck on this, read Luke 7:39 and Luke 5:30.)'

4 Would you think of inviting someone to your party who is despised by the rest of your group? Or who is not wealthy enough to return the invitation? Why/why not?

5 How can we put into practice the kind of hospitality that Jesus recommended? (Take note of any ideas which the group could try out.)

6 Is it ever right to feast if so many people in the world are starving?

WORSHIP

Gather round in a circle, with a place setting in the centre which has several different knives, forks, spoons, plates and glasses as if all ready for a feast. Sing together *Love is his Word* (HOAN) and let the singing fade into a time of silence.

Reader 1 Luke 6:32-36.

If you only love those who love you, what thanks do you deserve?

All Even 'sinners' love those who love them!

Reader 1 And if you happen to do good to those who do good to you, what thanks do you deserve?

All Even 'sinners' do that much!

Reader 1 And if you only lend to those you are sure will pay you back, what thanks do you deserve?

All Even 'sinners' lend to 'sinners' if they're getting the same amount back!

Reader 2 Instead, love your enemies and do good to them. Lend to them without any hope of getting anything back. And your reward will be great, and you will be children of the Most High God, because he is kind to the ungrateful and the wicked.

All So be merciful and compassionate, just as your Father is merciful and compassionate.

Sing together a song or chorus such as:
If anyone is thirsty (SOTS3)
My Lord, my Master (SOTS3)
The Lord's my Shepherd (HOAN)
Oh, come to the water (HOAN)

Reader 1 Father, we pray for all those who are rich and do not realise their need of you.

Silence

Reader 2 We pray for those who are rejected by society; for the unwanted and the unloved.

Silence

All Father, you have been so generous to us; help us to give freely and generously to others. Amen.

SESSION FOUR

Fasting

THINKING THINGS OUT

1 What is fasting? In small groups of two or three try this quiz, looking up the Bible references for the answers:
Q. Why did these people fast?
a. Joshua (Joshua 7:5-6).
b. David (2 Samuel 12:16, 22-23).
c. Ezra (Ezra 8:21-23).
d. Esther (Esther 4:15-16).
Q. Which of these fasts does Jesus disapprove of and why?
a. Matthew 6:17-18 *or* b. Matthew 6:16.
In the large group go through the quiz and write up the answers on a wall chart.

2 Why do people fast in our society? (Write these ideas down as well.)

3 What good is there in fasting? (Write down both good and bad points.)

To read together: John 13:12-17.

4 When Jesus washes his disciples' feet, he is giving them an example of willing, selfless service to others. What kind of 'fasting' does this suggest?

5 Plan a fast as an act of love and an exercise in self discipline. It need not necessarily be a fast from food, and it could be sponsored. It helps if it is communal and linked to practical help for others.

WORSHIP

Gather round in a circle with a cup of water placed in the centre and sing *Here I am, Lord* (SOTS 3). Let the singing fade into a time of silence.

Reader 1 John 13:4-9.

Jesus got up from the meal, took off his outer coat and wrapped a towel round his waist. Then he poured water into a basin and began to wash the disciples' feet and wipe them dry with the towel he was wearing. He came to Simon Peter, who said to him,

Reader 2 'Lord, are you going to wash my feet?'

Reader 3 Jesus answered him, 'At the moment you do not understand what I am doing, but later on you will.'

Reader 2 'Never!' said Peter, 'I will never have you washing my feet!'

Reader 3 'Unless I do wash your feet,' replied Jesus, 'you will not be able to share in my life.'

Reader 2 'In that case,' said Simon Peter, 'not just my feet, Lord, but my hands and my head as well!'

Sing together a song or chorus such as:
Here I am, Lord (SOTS3)
In the bleak mid winter (HOAN)
Make me a channel of your peace (HOAN)
O Lord, your tenderness (SOF 4)
Take my hands and make them (HOAN)

Reader 1 Father, we ask you to help us fast from all that is unloving and unkind,

All so that we enable others to share your banquet of joy and peace.

Reader 2 We ask you to give us your spirit of discipline,

All so that our lives are ruled by your law of love. Amen.

SESSION FIVE
Following the recipe

THINKING THINGS OUT

Have a number of cards with different ingredients written on each, and give one card to each person. They have to get together into groups whose ingredients make up a traditional dish for a festive occasion:

Christmas pudding — sultanas, suet, raisins, flour, apple etc.
Birthday cake — icing, candles, fruit, sugar, flour, eggs etc.
Christmas dinner — turkey, chestnut stuffing, roast potatoes, brussel sprouts, gravy etc.
Pancakes — eggs, milk, flour, salt, lemon, sugar.

1 Which of these dishes would you be able to cook without using a recipe?

2 What kind of things do recipes tell us? (Make a note of these things on a board or sheet of paper. Such things as knowing how much of something to use, how long to cook it for, the best order to mix things in etc.)

3 What general points about cooking do we need to know to be successful (and safe) in preparing food? (Note these down as well, e.g. hygiene, stirring to stop things sticking, clearing up as you go, etc.)

To read together: Matthew 5:14-16; John 13:34-35.

4 What is the spiritual 'recipe' in these readings, do you think?

5 God's kingdom of Love is what we are all helping to make. We are both ingredients and cooks! Look up these references and see how Jesus gives us practical help. You can link them with the points you made about cooking:
Matthew 10:16 (Take care).
Matthew 10:19-20; Luke 11:9-10 (What to do and when).
Matthew 6:12 (Clean up your mess!)

6 How can we keep in touch with the power we need?

WORSHIP

Gather round in a circle, and in the centre have an arrangement of an open Bible surrounded by a few cooking utensils. Sing together *Take me, Lord, use my life* (HOAN) and let the singing fade into a time of silence.

Reader 1 Luke 9:12-17.
It was late in the afternoon when the Twelve came to Jesus and said,

All 'Send the people away, so that they can go to the local villages and towns and find some food and accommodation there, because we are in a remote area here.'

Reader 1 But Jesus said to them,

Reader 2 'Give them something to eat yourselves.'

Reader 1 They answered,

All 'We have only got five loaves and two fishes — unless you mean we should go and buy food for all these people.'

Reader 1 There were about five thousand people there. Jesus said to his disciples,

Reader 2 'Get them to sit down in groups of fifty.'

Reader 1 They did so, and everyone sat down. Then Jesus took the five loaves and the two fishes, looked up to heaven and thanked God for them. He broke them up and gave them to his disciples so they could distribute them to the crowd.

All Everyone ate; and they all had as much as they wanted, with twelve basketfuls left over.

Sing together a song or chorus such as:
  Love is something if you give it away (Alleluya!)
  Freely, freely (HOAN)
  If God is for us (SOTS)
  Let there be love shared among you (SOTS3)

Reader 1 Father, we offer you ourselves for you to use;

All take our time,
  our energy,
  our strength,
  our weakness,
  our talents and skills.

Reader 1 Make us into the kind of people you want us to be,

All and then use us, Lord, for the good of your world. Amen.

SESSION SIX

Celebration!

THINKING THINGS OUT

[1] In small groups of two or three make shopping lists on the resource sheets for different kinds of celebrations:

A welcome home celebration.

A 3rd birthday.

A wedding.

[2] In the large group, share the lists and let the others guess from the lists the kind of celebration being planned.

[3] Why do we nearly always include food for times of celebration? (Write the suggestions down — such things as food being a basic human requirement; we all eat so no-one will be left out; food celebrates our existence etc.)

To read together: Exodus 12:25-27; Mark 14:22-25; 1 Corinthians 11:26-27.

[4] What are the people of Israel celebrating at the Passover?

[5] What was Jesus celebrating at the Last Supper?

[6] What kind of freedom was Jesus offering his followers in this new covenant?

[7] What are Christians celebrating at Holy Communion?

[8] Why is it so important to be well prepared for Communion?

WORSHIP

This should take the form of a celebration of the Eucharist, if possible using the bread which has been made, and the altar set.

Suggested music:
  God and man at table are sat down (HOAN)
  Blest are you, Lord (SOTS3)
  Gifts of bread and wine (HOAN)
  In bread we bring you, Lord (HOAN)
  Be not afraid (MSOTS)
  I give my hands (HOAN)
Suggested readings:
  Exodus 16:9-16; Luke 24:13, 28-35.
Suggested Psalm:
  Oh, how good is the Lord (HOAN).

Invite the rest of the parish to share in this celebration and offer refreshments afterwards (if there are practical problems with using the bread the group has made for the Eucharist itself, it can be distributed now as 'Agape' bread — Orthodox Christians distribute the unconsecrated portion of the bread after the Eucharist) so that people can see what the group has been up to during the previous sessions in this Unit. This is also a good opportunity to launch the parish recipe book!

GAMES

FOOD MATCH

This is a useful game for getting people to talk to one another. Each person is given a label and has to find her/his partner(s) by finding a matching label on someone else. You could have combinations such as bacon and eggs, fish and chips, sausages and mash etc., or titles of dishes which involve two or more words, such as chilli con carne, fruit salad, ice cream, toad in the hole etc.

FEEDING BLINDFOLD

This messy game is always both popular and revolting. For the strong of stomach, it involves a blindfolded person attempting to feed someone with a suitably sloppy food such as very wobbly jelly. Protective clothing is advisable!

GUESS WHAT

Another blindfold game. This time a group prepares an assortment of different foods and those blindfolded have to guess what they are by relying entirely on taste. This is an interesting game as it quickly becomes apparent that we must rely heavily on sight to know what we are eating most of the time. Similar textures are often confused.

RACES

There are plenty of traditional 'food' races and they are good fun to try. There is a pancake race, for instance, in which the home-made pancakes must be tossed at least three times before the finish. The egg and spoon race demands both speed and a steady hand, and the potato race involves picking up a trail of potatoes, one by one, and filling a sack with them. You could of course invent your own variations on these; how about a jelly race, a potato peeling race or sandwich making race?

ROLL FOR A BITE

In the centre of the circle have a bar of chocolate, together with a knife and fork and two sets of crazy clothes. These should include heavyweight gloves, some kind of hat, a coat, scarf and pair of sunglasses. Take turns to throw the dice, and whenever a 6 is thrown the person who threw it dashes into the centre, dresses up in the clothes and attempts to eat some of the chocolate with a knife and fork. As soon as another 6 is thrown, the next person comes to take over.

FLOUR CAKE

Press flour into a pudding basin so that it keeps its shape when you turn it out. Place this on the floor in the centre of the circle. Each person in turn cuts a slice off the flour cake, being careful not to demolish it completely. The one who manages to flatten the cake is the loser and has to pay some kind of forfeit. A variation of this game is to have a coin in the flour, and whoever uncovers the coin must pick it out with their teeth!

BOBBING FOR APPLES

Apples are bobbing about in a large bowl of water, and you try and pick them out with your teeth; hands must be clasped firmly behind you throughout. A variation of this is to have doughnuts threaded on string, fairly high above the group. If the ends of the string are held by two extremely fidgety people, the task is much harder and more fun.

PART TWO: RESOURCE SHEETS

*Note: the Resource Sheets which follow may be photocopied for use in youth groups or schools in conjunction with **Growing**. Each activity sheet, headed by the title of the session of **Growing** to which it relates, is printed facing its corresponding 'Worship' text. Both can be photocopied onto one side of an A3 sheet, which can then be folded, or they can be backed up on an A4 sheet.*

Have you heard. . . ?

TO TALK ABOUT . . .

1 In the game of Chinese Whispers, what happened to the message as it was passed on?

2 How does the same kind of thing happen with rumours?

3 If you wanted to make sure a message would be passed on accurately, how would you do it?

4 Are there any stories which have been passed down in your family which you especially enjoy? If so, perhaps you would like to share them with the person sitting next to you now.

5 Which do you enjoy most – news about events or people?

6 If you read a false rumour about yourself in a newspaper, how would you feel and what would you do?

7 If we didn't have a written language, why do you think we might value old people as especially important in our community?

8 During the week, ask an elderly relative or friend what s/he can remember about schools, heating, children's jobs, food, homes, games etc. when s/he was a child.

Have you heard?

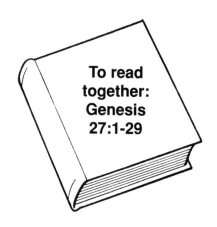

To read together: Genesis 27:1-29

WORSHIP

Sing together *Joshua fought the battle of Jericho* and *Rise and shine*, so that you are keeping the tradition of enjoying the old family stories of the Bible. After the singing have a time of silence.

Reader 1   Exodus 12:23-27a
The Lord will pass through the country killing
the Egyptians, and when he sees the blood on your
doorframes, he will pass over and refuse to let
the Destroyer come into your houses to harm you.
Both you and your descendants must obey these
rules for ever.

Reader 2   And when you arrive at the land which God will
give you, just as he has promised, you must keep this ritual.
When your children ask you,

Half   'What does this ritual mean?'

Reader 2   you will reply,

Other half   'It is the Passover sacrifice in honour of the Lord,
who passed over the houses of the Israelites in Egypt,
killing the Egyptians but sparing us.'

Sing together a song or chorus.

Reader 1   Father, we pray for all who work for newspapers,
or in broadcasting.

Silence

All   Help them to give information with honesty
and sensitivity. Open our hearts so that we are
responsive to the needs of our world.

1:1

Heroes and idols

Music	Sport	Goodness	Power	Badness

Who do you think are the heroes of today?

To read together: Judges 16:1-22

TO TALK ABOUT . . .

1 Who are our society's heroes? Write their names in the spaces above.

2 Why do we like having heroes and anti-heroes?

3 We sometimes talk of 'hero worship'. How is this similar to, or different from, worship of God?

4 What is the difference between a hero and an idol?

5 You can imagine what the newspapers would make of Samson! What headlines and sub-headlines might there be if Delilah sold her story to the press?

6 In what ways would Samson appeal to the public?

7 Do you think he was using his gift of strength in the best way?

8 Does our society tempt us to use our gifts to become rich, rather than for a more valuable goal?

9 Can you think of any times when people have decided to use their talents for a good cause? Share these with the group.

WORSHIP

Sing together *Thine be the glory* and let the singing fade into a time of silence.

Reader 1   1 Kings 3:23-28.
    King Solomon said thoughtfully,

Reader 2   'One of you women says. "This living son is mine –
    yours is dead", while the other woman claims, "No. that's
    not true – your son is the dead one – mine is alive!" '

Reader 1   The king asked for a sword.
    When they brought it to him he declared,

Reader 2   'Split the living child in two, and give half
    to one woman and half to the other.'

Reader 1   At that the real mother cried out to the king, deeply
    distressed at the thought of her son coming to harm.

Reader 3   'O my lord king, I would rather you gave the child
    to the other woman than kill it!'

Reader 1   But the other woman said,

Reader 4   'No, let neither of us have it. Cut it in half.'

Reader 1   Then King Solomon gave his decision.

Reader 2   'Don't kill the child. but give him to the first woman;
    she must be his real mother.'

Reader 1   All Israel heard about the way the king had dealt
    with the problem, and they had great respect for him.
    They could see that he possessed God's wisdom,
    which enabled him to settle disputes fairly.

Sing together a song or chorus.

Reader 1   Father, we pray for all famous people
    and well-known stars.

Silence

All   May they not be spoilt and damaged by their fame.
    Help us to remember that all we have comes from you.
    We offer ourselves and our talents and skills and weaknesses
    for you to use for the good of your world. Amen.

1:2

Gloom, doom, hope and glory

Search for the prophets – Look in the Bible for their names

```
H B H A I A S I R U H N
O A O H P O L C D I A W
S C B J M L V A G H G H
E H A A F E N E U A G A
A J D N K I K M O I A I
D O I O E K D T Y M I N
G N A L M E U B Q E S A
C A H E D Z A K L R Q H
X H F J O E L R A E B P
M I C A H I J W Z J S E
K U P H A I R A H C E Z
N M A L A C H I M Y T V
```

TO TALK ABOUT . . .

1 Who are the prophets in the Bible?
Find their names in the Wordsearch grid above

2 What do you think a prophet does? This may
be different from what you would expect, so
these references will help you: Isaiah 6:8;
Isaiah 7:10; Ezekiel 3:22; Hosea 1:2.

3 Why do you think the prophets were not usually
popular? Are such people popular today?

4 How did Jonah react to being called by God?

5 If you don't want to do something you know you
ought to do, are you ever tempted to go as far
as possible in the opposite direction?

6 How did God use Jonah as his messenger
even while he was running away?

7 Dare we speak out for what is right? Even if it
means standing alone? Even if it brings insults
and persecution?

8 False prophets say only what people want to
hear. When does that happen in our society?

9 How can we be sure it really is God who is
calling us? Look at these references to help
you: Matthew 12:33-35; Matthew 7:15-20.

To read
together:
Jonah 1

WORSHIP

Sing together *Tell out my soul* and let the singing fade
into silence.

Reader 1 Jeremiah 20:8-9 (Jeremiah complains to the Lord).
Whenever I speak I have to moan and cry out,

Reader 2 'Destruction! Ruin!'
Reader 1 The word of the Lord which I proclaim,
makes me ridiculed and insulted every day.
So I think to myself,

Reader 2 'I will ignore the Lord and refuse to speak any more
in his name.'

Reader 1 But if I do this, his word burns like a fire deep inside
my bones, until I am exhausted from holding it in,
and can no longer stop myself from speaking out.

Sing together a song or chorus.

Reader 3 Matthew 7:21.
Not all those who say to me. 'Lord, Lord,'
will enter into the kingdom of heaven,
but only the person who does the will
of my Father in heaven.

All Father, when you speak to us,
help us to listen;
when you call us,
give us courage to follow;
speak through our thoughts,
our words and our actions,
so that we do your will. Amen.

1:3

Rediscovered treasure

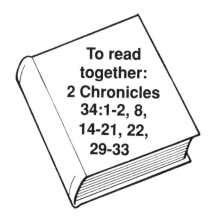

TO TALK ABOUT . . .

1   How did you feel when you realised you had lost something important? How did your body react?

2   Suppose you had just found, buried in your bedroom, something you were supposed to have dealt with ages ago. How might you feel, and what might you do?

3   It took the very young king, Josiah, to start cleaning the country up. What did his workmen find buried in a corner of the temple storeroom?

4   How did Josiah react to the discovery?

5   Imagine you are King Josiah. How would you go about putting things right, now that the book of Moses, containing God's Law, has been found?

6   Compare your ideas with the way Josiah himself tackled the problem.

7   Recently we have discovered the vital importance to our survival of rain forests. Having discovered the truth, and realised the harm we are doing, how should we react?

8   How do we feel, and what should we do, when we realise we have not been living as Jesus told us to?

To read together: 2 Chronicles 34:1-2, 8, 14-21, 22, 29-33

WORSHIP

Sing together *The King of love my shepherd is* and let the singing fade into a time of silence.

Reader 1   Luke 15:11-20 (the lost son, paraphrased).
There was once a man who had two sons.
The younger one said to him,

Reader 2   'Father. give me my share of the property now.'

Reader 1   So the man divided his property between his two
sons . . . The second son spent everything he had.
Then a severe famine spread over that country,
and he was left without a thing. So he went to work
looking after pigs. He wished he could fill himself
with the bean pods the pigs ate, but no one gave him
anything to eat. At last he came to his senses and said,

Reader 2   'All my father's hired workers have more than they
can eat. and here am I about to starve! I will get up
and go to my father and say. "Father, I have sinned
against God and against you. I am no longer fit to be
called your son: treat me as one of your hired workers".'

Reader 1   So he got up and started back to his father.

Sing together a song or chorus.

Reader 3   Father, we pray for all who have wandered away
from you; for all who feel they have travelled too far
to be forgiven.

Silence

All   Give us all deep sorrow for our sin.
and the reassurance of your forgiveness. Amen.

1:4

It's Gospel!

To read
together:
John 9

TO TALK ABOUT . . .

1 Ask the different characters how they felt and what went through their minds when Jesus asked who had touched him. (Include Jesus.)

2 If you were in the crowd, how did you feel about the woman? How did your feelings change when Jesus told her to go in peace, because her faith had made her well?

3 Why do you think the woman touched Jesus when he was in a milling crowd?

4 Why did that touch feel different to Jesus from the usual pushing of the crowd?

5 What kind of person does Jesus appear to be, from our knowledge of him in the gospels?

6 Why did many of the Pharisees find it so difficult to believe that Jesus was the Son of God?

7 Why did he attract such a huge following of people, do you think?

WORSHIP

Sing together *Father, we love you* and let the singing fade into a time of silence.

Reader 1 John 9:35-38.
Jesus heard that the man had been thrown out, and when he had found him he asked him,

Reader 2 'Do you believe in the Son of God?'

Reader 1 The man answered,

Reader 3 'Who is he, sir? Tell me, so that I may believe in him.'

Reader 1 Jesus said to him,

Reader 2 'You have seen him already.
He is the one talking with you now.'

Reader 3 'Lord, I do believe!'

Reader 1 said the man, and he flung himself down before Jesus.

Sing a song or chorus.

Reader 1 Lord, open our eyes to see you clearly;

All open our hearts to trust you more.

Reader 1 Lord, open our ears to hear you speaking;

All open our minds to understand.

Reader 1 Lord, you walked as a person among us;

All walk with us every step of our way. Amen.

1:5

75

Good news! Good news!

Look at the picture and read the article. Now . . .

Questions Score	1	2	3
How do you rate:			
1 The truth of the headlines?			
2 The relevance of the picture?			
3 The entertainment value?			
4 The news content?			
5 The usefulness?			
6 The harm?			

TO TALK ABOUT . . .

1 How do the articles give a false or destructive message?

2 Why do you think the writer chose to put this slant on the facts?

3 Should Christians refuse to take part in such things as propaganda, advertising or the 'gutter' press? Give your reasons.

4 What is the good news that Peter and John are so excited about?

5 How have they shown their message in action, as well as in words?

6 Why are the members of the Council so surprised at Peter and John's speech?

7 What had Jesus promised his followers about speaking up for the truth? (Mark 13:11.)

8 How do we sometimes give a confused message about God's saving love for the world?

9 Having seen the kind of person Jesus was in the gospels, how do you think Jesus wants you to follow him today?

To read together: Acts 4:8-20

WORSHIP

Sing together *God's Spirit is in my heart* and let the singing fade into a time of silence.

Reader 1   Acts 16:25-32.
   At midnight, Paul and Silas, who were praying,
   sang a hymn to God and the other prisoners listened
   to them. Suddenly there was a violent earth tremor,
   enough to shake the foundations of the prison.
   All the doors were flung open and all the prisoners'
   fetters snapped.

Reader 2   The gaoler, jerked out of sleep, saw all the open
   prison doors and drew his sword to kill himself,
   because he thought all the prisoners must have escaped.
   But Paul shouted out at the top of his voice,

Reader 3   'You mustn't do yourself any harm! We are all here!'

Reader 1   The gaoler asked for some lights, and then rushed in,
   where he fell at the feet of Paul and Silas,
   trembling with terror. Then he led them out
   and said to them,

Reader 4   'Sirs, what do I have to do to be saved?'

Reader 1   They replied,

Reader 3   'Believe in the Lord Jesus, the Christ,
   and both you and all your family will be saved.'

Reader 1   And they explained the word of the Lord to him
   and to everyone in his house.

Sing together a song or chorus.

Reader 2   Father, we praise you with all our being.

All   Use us to spread the good news of your love! Amen.

1:6

77

Setting off

Things to pack

TO TALK ABOUT . . .

1   Imagine you are setting out on a pilgrimage. Which things will you pack? Number the items in order of importance and pack them in the backpack.

2   Now you are told there is a restriction on your luggage, and as a group you must choose only THREE items. Which will you choose and why?

3   What did Abram take with him on his journey?

4   Find out where Haran is and work out how far it is from there to Canaan. How long do you think it might have taken them?

5   What do we need to set off on our pilgrimage to heaven? Read Ephesians 6:14-18 to give you some ideas.

To read together: Genesis 12:1-6 Ephesians 6:14-18

WORSHIP

Sing together *Shalom* .

Reader 1   Matthew 2:1-2.
When Jesus had been born at Bethlehem in Judaea
during the reign of King Herod,
some wise men from a country in the east
came into Jerusalem asking,

Reader 2   'Where is the new-born king of the Jews?
We saw the rising of his star,
and have come here to pay our respects.'

All   Lord, guide us on our journey to find you.

Reader 3   After their interview with Herod they left,
and the star whose rising they had witnessed now
moved in front of them until it stopped over
the place where the child was.

All   Lord, guide us on our journey to find you.

Reader 1   They were overjoyed to see the star,
and, having come into the house,
they saw the child with Mary, his mother.
Falling to their knees
they honoured him with great reverence.
Then, from their treasures, they offered him gifts
of gold, frankincense and myrrh.

Sing together a worship chorus.

All   Send us out into the world in peace
to live and work to your praise and glory. Amen

2:1

Finding the way

To read
together:
Ephesians 5:1-12
Hebrews 13:1-6

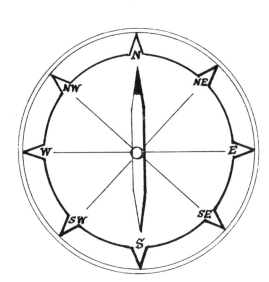

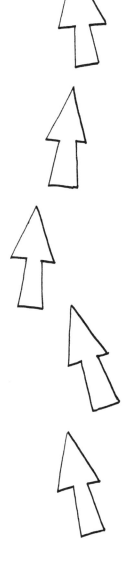

TO TALK ABOUT . . .

1   Sort the resource material into two lots – one lot
which helps us find our way on our spiritual
journey through life, and the other lot which
hinders us.

2   Put the helpful lot in order of importance to you
as a Christian.

3   How do the words in the readings link with the
constructive suggestions offered in our
role plays?

WORSHIP

Sing together *Ubi Caritas* letting the singing fade
into a time of silence.

Reader 1 John 13:12-17.
> When Jesus had washed their feet, and put his coat
> back on, he went and settled down with them again.

Reader 2 He said to them. 'Do you understand what I have
> done to you? You call me Lord and Teacher.
> and rightly so, because that is what I am.
> If I, then, as your Lord and Teacher, washed your
> feet, you must wash the feet of one another. I have
> set you an example, for you to copy the way I have
> behaved towards you.'

All 'In all truth I tell you, no slave is more important
> than his master, nor any messenger more important
> than the one who sends him.'

Reader 1 'Now that you understand this truth, how blessed
> you will be if you put it into practice!'

Sing a chorus or hymn together.

Reader 2 Lord Jesus, you are the Way;

All guide us to walk always in the path of your love.
> Amen.

2:2

Mountains, forests and deserts

My most difficult, scary journey ever was . . .

To read together:
Isaiah 49:10
Matthew 5:10-12

TO TALK ABOUT . . .

1 Tell each other about the most difficult, uncomfortable or scary journey you have ever made. Write about it in the space above.

2 List some of the things that helped keep you going when times were rough.

3 Have you ever found you have been given help, just when you were about to give up? Were you given practical help, encouragement, appreciation, or a bit of breathing space, for instance?

4 No doubt there have also been times when you have found it very hard to be a Christian. Talk about such times; you will probably be surprised to find how many of you have had similar problems.

5 There! God never promised us a rose garden, or even a peaceful life, according to this reading. And he even expects us to be happy about it. List some people who have lived/are living like this. Would you be prepared to be persecuted or insulted or ridiculed for your faith, do you think?

WORSHIP

Sing together *Walk with me, O my Lord*. Let the singing fade into a time of silence.

Reader 1 Mark 13:7-13.
When you hear of wars and rumours of wars,
don't be disturbed. This must all happen,
but it does not mean that the end has arrived.
Nation will fight against nation, and kingdom
against kingdom; there will be earthquakes
in some places, and famines. These are like
the beginning of labour pains at a birth.

Reader 2 But you yourselves must be on your guard.
You will be handed over to sanhedrins:
you will be beaten in synagogues, and on my
account you will be put on trial before governors
and kings, so as to witness to them about me.
It is first necessary for the Good News to be
proclaimed to every country.

Reader 3 Lord. we pray for all who are being tortured
or punished for their faith at the moment.

Silence

Reader 3 Jesus, please help them;

All   give them your strength.

Reader 4 But when you are arrested and handed over,
don't be anxious beforehand about what you should
say; when the time comes just say whatever is then
given to you, for what you say will come not from
you but from the Holy Spirit.

Reader 3 Lord, we pray for the right words when we
are asked about what we believe.

Silence

Reader 3 Jesus, fill us with your Spirit.

All   and use us to show your love.

Sing together a chorus or song.

Reader 3 Lord, in your strength

All   we shall be strong. Amen.

2:3

Food for the journey

Wrapper sorting

Basic nutritious food	Luxury/junk food

To read together: Exodus 16:11-15 Luke 9:12-17

TO TALK ABOUT . . .

1 Sort the labels into two lots: the first for those foods which are basic to a nutritious diet; the second for those which are either luxury or junk food.

2 What happens to your body when it needs an intake of food – how does it let you know?

3 What happens if our bodies are deprived of the food they need?

4 God uses what is offered in the desert and in a lunch box, so that many thousands can be fed. What do you think the people learnt about God through being fed like this?

5 If we can only offer a little of our time/money/skills is it worth offering at all?

6 How does God make sure we can be regularly fed on our spiritual journey?

7 Look again at Question 3, and discuss the same question about spiritual feeding.

WORSHIP

Sing *Oh, come to the Water* or *As I went a-walking one morning in Spring* and let the singing fade into a time of silence.

Reader 1 John 6: 33-35.
  The bread of God is the bread which comes down
  from heaven and is giving life to the world.

All   'Sir,' they said to him, 'always give us this bread.'

Reader 2 Jesus replied, 'I am the bread of life;
  whoever comes to me shall never be hungry,
  and whoever believes in me
  shall never ever be thirsty.'

Sing together a chorus or song.

Reader 1 Heavenly father, feed us on our journey

All   and use us to feed others. Amen.

2:4

Getting lost

TO TALK ABOUT . . .

1 What do you have to do in a maze if you go the wrong way? Have you ever tried a full-sized maze? Tell the others about it.

2 Have you ever read the map wrongly and got yourself lost? How did you get back to the right place?

3 How would you say this man had lost his way?

4 Why didn't the father just send him away, or treat him as a hired servant?

5 What can we discover about God's attitude to us when we go wrong?

6 How is Jesus suggesting we should behave to those who wrong us in any way?

7 Do you think it is possible to keep forgiving like this? How can we improve our 'stamina' in forgiving?

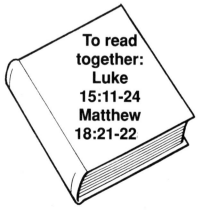

To read together: Luke 15:11-24 Matthew 18:21-22

WORSHIP

Sing *Spirit of the living God* and let the singing fade into a time of silence.

Reader 1 John 14:5-6.
> Thomas says to Jesus, 'Lord, we do not know where you are going, so how are we able to know the way?'

Reader 2 Jesus answers him, 'I am the Way;
> I am the truth and I am life.
> No one comes to the Father except through me.'

Reader 3 Isaiah 53:5-6.
> Yet he was wounded because of our wrongdoing;
> he was crushed because of our evil. He suffered
> the punishment which brings us healing, we have
> been made whole by the bruises he endured.

All   Like sheep, we had all scattered and become lost,
> each wandering off our own way.

Reader 3 And the Lord laid on him the punishment

All   which all of us deserved.

Sing together a chorus or hymn.

Reader 1 Father, if we wander from your way,

All   bring us back. Amen.

2:5

Journey's end

TO TALK ABOUT . . .

1 Tell one another how you think you might react if you were told you had only one year to live? What about one week, or one hour?

2 In what ways might your reactions be different if you were 30 years older?

3 In the space to the right of these questions make a list of the qualities of heaven that we do know about. (The parables of the mustard seed, the yeast, the hidden treasure, and the net may help. You'll find these in Matthew 13.)

4 If we know that our life doesn't end with physical death, how does that affect our way of living?

5 How will it change the way we react when things go wrong?

6 How will it affect our willingness to suffer for our faith?

Heaven is . . .

To read together:
Romans 8:18,37-39
Revelation 7:13-17

WORSHIP

Sing together *Jubilate everybody* and enjoy dancing as well as singing.

Reader 1   1 Corinthians 13: 8-10, 12.
   Love never falls away. Where there are prophecies,
   they will come to an end; where there are tongues,
   they will be silent; where there is knowledge,
   it will vanish. For our understanding is only partial,
   and our prophesying is only partial; but once
   perfection comes, then all that is partial
   will come to an end.

Reader 2   For now we see only dim, confusing reflections
   in a mirror, but then we shall see face to face.
   Now I understand only in part, but then I shall
   understand fully, just as I am fully known and understood.

Sing together a chorus or hymn.

Reader 3   Father, during our pilgrimage through life
   prepare us for heaven,

All   and welcome us into your everlasting kingdom.
   Amen.

2:6

Scared of the dark

DARKNESS

What is dangerous about the darkness?

Why do you think so many children are frightened by the dark?

LIGHT

What is comforting/safe about the light?

In what way is light useful?

TO TALK ABOUT . . .

1 What is frightening or dangerous about the darkness?

2 Why are many children scared of the dark?

3 What is comforting/safe about the light?

4 In what way is light useful?

5 In the light (!) of what you have been talking about, what do you think the writer of Genesis was saying about the character of God?

6 Why do you think the creation story begins with total darkness being changed into light?

7 In what way/s are the two passages you have read similar?

8 How do our own discussion points about light fit in with what John wrote?

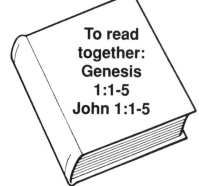

To read together: Genesis 1:1-5 John 1:1-5

WORSHIP

Sing together *The light of Christ,* accompanied with instruments if you have them. Let the singing fade into a time of silence.

Reader   Genesis 1:1-5.
In the beginning God created
the heavens and the earth.
Now the earth was
a shapeless emptiness,
there was darkness over
the surface of the ocean depths,
and the Spirit of God breathing
over the waters. God said,
'Let there be light' – and there
was light. God saw
that the light was good,
and God separated the light from
the darkness. God called
the light 'day' and the darkness
he called 'night'. Evening came,
and morning came – the first day.

Sing together a chorus or hymn. During the singing, each person in turn goes and lights a candle from the central one, and places it on the floor in the centre of the group.

Reader   Let us bring into the light of
God's love the dark areas of
our world.
– those who are scared or worried
– those with no home to sleep in.

Silence

All   God of love: shine in
the darkness

Reader   Into his healing light
we bring
– those waiting in
casualty departments

– all victims of crimes
and accidents.

Silence

All   God of love:
shine in the darkness.

Reader   Into his welcoming light
we bring
– those whose lives
are confused
– those who are searching
for life's meaning.

Silence

All   God of light: shine in
the darkness.

Reader   John 1:1-5.

All   In the beginning the Word
already existed: the Word was
with God and the Word
was God. This Word was with
God right from the beginning.
Through this, everything
was done; without this,
not one thing that has been made
could have been made.
In this Word was life, and the life
was the light of humankind.
And the light shines in
the darkness,
and the darkness has never
quenched it.

Reader   In the darkness
of selfishness and greed,
go out and shine as lights
of God's love.

All   In the power of our loving
God, we will.

3:1

91

Warnings and guides

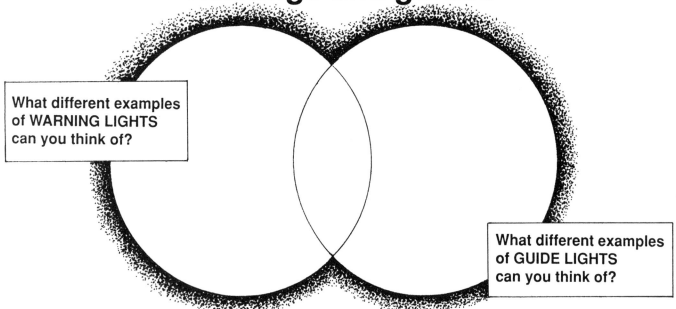

What different examples of WARNING LIGHTS can you think of?

What different examples of GUIDE LIGHTS can you think of?

TO TALK ABOUT . . .

1 What different examples of warning lights can you think of?

2 What different examples of guide lights can you think of?

3 In fours, imagine that two of you are strict Pharisees and the other two are followers of Jesus. What things in Jesus' character and behaviour have convinced you that he is the light of the world? Try to show the Pharisees that Jesus is the light they have been waiting for.

4 Look again at how some 'guide' lights also become effective 'warning' lights. How does God's light sometimes become a warning light for us?

5 What if God's light shows up areas of our life we prefer to keep dark? What *might* we do? What *should* we do?

6 Why did the Pharisees see Jesus' light as a threat?

Role Play

**You and your partner are followers of Jesus.
Try to persuade two Pharisees that Jesus is really the Messiah they are waiting for!**

**To read together:
Isaiah 9:2
Matthew 11:2-6
John 8:12-13**

WORSHIP

Sing a chorus together such as *Do not be afraid,* accompanied with instruments if you have them. Let the singing fade into a time of silence.

3 Readers together   Isaiah 9:2-3.
    The people who were walking in
    darkness have seen a great light.
    On those living in a land of deep
    shadow, brilliant light has dawned.
    You have enlarged the nation,
    O Lord, and deepened their joy.

Sing together a hymn. During the singing, each person in turn goes and lights a candle from the central one, and places it on the floor in the centre of the group.

Reader   Let us bring into the light of
    God's love some of the dark areas
    of our world:
    – those whose lives are in danger
    – those who are imprisoned
      or exiled.

All   God of light:
    shine in the darkness.

Silence

Reader   Into his healing light
    we bring
    – those undergoing surgery
    – any people in pain at
      the moment.

Silence

All   God of light:
    shine in the darkness.

Reader   Into his welcoming light
    we bring
    – those who have lost their way
    – all who have difficult decisions
      to make.

Silence

All   God of light:
    shine in the darkness.

Reader 1   Matthew 11 :2-6.
    Now John the Baptist, who was in
    prison, heard about what Christ
    was doing, and sent two
    of his own disciples to ask him,

All   'Are you the One
    whose coming was promised,
    or should we be expecting
    someone else?'

Reader 2   Jesus answered them,
    'Go back and report to John
    what you hear and see –
    blind people can see again,
    the lame ones are able to walk
    about, those with skin diseases
    are cleansed, and the deaf are
    hearing; dead people are being
    brought to life and the poor are
    personally given the good news.

All   'What blessings there are for
    those who do not think of me as a
    stumbling block!'

Readers I and 2   Jesus is the light
    of the world.

All   We will walk in his light.

3:2

The darkness of evil

GREED
DESTRUCTION
MISERY

TO TALK ABOUT . . .

1   What different areas of 'darkness' have we collected?

2   Try to get behind the actual crime committed to see the spiritual darkness, or sin, that made such evil possible. (For example, in a case of violent robbery, might it be greed? influence of videos? poor upbringing? mental illness? selfishness?)

3   Is it possible to become better people through our own efforts?

4   How does it help if God is prepared to forgive us?

5   What else does God offer us to lighten the darkness?

Crafty Idea!

Use all the newspaper and magazine pictures to make a collage of misery, greed and destruction.

To read together:
John 14:15-16, 27
Matthew 11:28
Galatians 5:19-25

WORSHIP

Sing together *Nada te turbe, nada te espante* and let the singing fade into a time of quietness.

Reader 1 Jeremiah 4:22.
   The Lord says,
   'My people are fools –
   they do not know me.
   They are behaving childishly;
   they have no understanding.
   They are so smart at doing
       what is evil,
   but useless at doing what is good.'

Reader 2 Isaiah 43:1.
   But now, Israel,
   the Lord who created
   and formed you speaks to you
   and says, 'Do not be afraid,
   for I have redeemed you;
   I have called you by name –
   you are mine.'

Sing together a hymn. During the singing, each person in turn goes and lights a candle from the central one, and places it on the floor in the centre of the group.

Reader Let us bring into the light of
   God's love the dark areas o
   our world:
   – the quarrelling
       and heated arguments
   – all who long for revenge.

All God of light:
   shine in the darkness.

Silence

Reader Into his healing light
   we bring
   – all victims of attack

   – those wounded
       or disabled through war.

Silence

All God of light:
   shine in the darkness.

Reader Into his welcoming light
   we bring
   – all who work for peace
   – all who need encouragement.

Silence

All God of light:
   shine in the darkness.

Reader Psalm 121.

All I lift up my eyes
   to the mountains;
   where does my help come from?
   My help comes from the Lord,
   who made heaven and earth.
   He will not let your foot slip –
   he who protects you
   will not fall asleep.
   In fact, he who watches over Israel
   never dozes or sleeps.
   He is right by your side
   to shade you,
   so that the sun will not burn you
   during the day, nor the moon
   during the night. The Lord protects
   you from all harm, and keeps you
   safe. He will watch over
   all your comings and goings
   both now and for ever.

Reader If the Lord is with us,

All who shall be against us!

3:3

In the dark

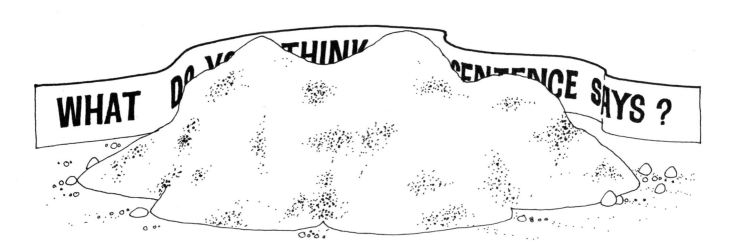

WHAT DO YOU THINK SENTENCE SAYS ?

TO TALK ABOUT . . .

1 How many words did you need to see before you could understand the message?

2 In a way, these readings are like different words in our secret mesage. How do they fit in with what we know of Jesus?

3 What message do you think they add up to make?

4 How was God gradually revealing this message in the many years before Jesus was born? (If you're stuck, see Romans 1:2-4.)

5 How do you think Philip managed to help the Ethiopian understand what he was reading?

Get in on the act!

In groups of 3 or 4, think about what things Philip might say to the Ethiopian, and what questions the Ethiopian might ask Philip. Now act it all out.

To read together:
Daniel 7:13-14
Micah 5:2
Isaiah 60:3
Isaiah 53:5

WORSHIP

Sing together *Here I am Lord* and let the singing fade into a time of silence.

Reader 1   Daniel 7:13-14.
As I was gazing at this vision
in the night I saw in front of me
what looked like a human being,
coming on the clouds of heaven.
He approached the One who lives
for ever and was led into
his presence. To him was given
authority, honour and kingly
power, and the people of all
nations, races and languages
served him. His reign lasts for ever,
it will never pass away; his
kingdom will never be destroyed.

Sing together a song. During the singing. each person in turn goes and lights a candle from the central one, and places it on the floor in the centre of the group.

Reader 2   Let us bring into the light
of God's love the dark areas
of our world
– those who have never yet heard
   of his love
– those who live constantly
   in terror.

Silence

All   God of love:
shine in the darkness.

Reader 3   Into his healing light
we bring
– those whose minds are confused
   by age or illness
– all those in hospital.

Silence

All   God of love:
shine in the darkness.

Reader 4   Into his welcoming light
we bring
– the newly born
– the newly baptised.

Silence

All   God of light:
shine in the darkness.

Reader 1   Mark 8:27-29.

All   Jesus and his disciples
went out into the villages
of Caesarea Philippi.
And on the way
he asked his disciples,
'Who do people say I am?'
'Some say you are John
the baptiser,' they answered,
'some that you are Elijah,
and others that you are one
of the prophets.'

Reader 1   'But what about you?'
he asked them
'Who do you say I am?'

Reader 2   Peter answered him.
'You are God's anointed one –
the Christ.'

Reader 1   Lord, to whom else
would we go?

All   You alone have the words
that give eternal life.

3:4

97

Quality lightbulbs

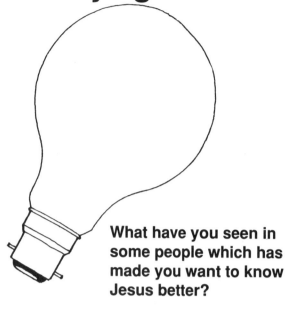

What have you seen in some people which has made you want to know Jesus better?

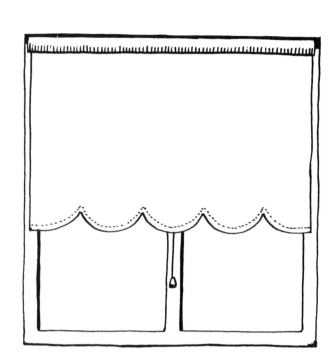

What kind of behaviour has given you a bad impression of Christians?

TO TALK ABOUT . . .

1   What qualities have you seen in some people which have made you want to know Jesus better?

2   What kind of behaviour has given you a bad impression of Christians?

3   On the light bulb above write the qualities which you have found 'shining' Christians have. On the blind, write the qualities which turn you or your friends away from Jesus.

4   What qualities did Jesus say would bring lasting blessing or happiness? (You may need to read Matthew 5:1-12, John 13:34-35.)

5   Why do you think real loving often involves getting hurt?

6   What will be the consequences if only a very few people shine with Christ's light in the world?

**To read together:
Matthew 5:14-16
Matthew 5:1-12
John 13:34-35**

WORSHIP

Sing together a chorus such as *Freely freely* and let the singing fade into a time of shared peace and quietness.

Reader 1 Matthew 5:14-15.
You are the light of the world. It is impossible for a city situated on a hill to be concealed; nor would you light a lamp and put it under a bowl, but on the lampstand where it will give light to everyone in the house.

Sing together a song or chorus. During the singing, each person in turn goes and lights a candle from the central one, and places it on the floor in the centre of the group.

Reader 3 Let us bring into the light of God's love
  – the wasted opportunities for showing care
  – the selfishness which blocks God's channels of love.

Silence

All God of love: shine in the darkness.

Reader 4 Into his healing light we bring
  – the prejudiced and resentful
  – those in pain which is wearing them down.

Silence

All God of love: shine in the darkness.

Reader 5 Into his welcoming light we bring
  – the disillusioned and disappointed
  – those driven from Christ by unhelpful Christian witness.

Silence

All God of light: shine in the darkness.

Reader 1 Happy are those whose greatest desire
  is to do what God requires;

All God will satisfy them fully!

Reader 2 Jesus is the light of the world.

All We will walk in his light!

3:5

Walk in the light

How did you feel during the walk?

How did it feel when the blindfold was taken off?

Make a list of 4 or 5 situations you have heard/seen/read about, where you feel people have 'blinded' themselves to what is right and just.

Have you ever felt frustrated because someone else couldn't 'see' what you mean?

To read together: Mark 8:22-25

TO TALK ABOUT . . .

1. How did you feel during the walk when you were blindfolded?

2. How did it feel when the blindfold was taken off?

3. Have you ever felt frustrated because someone couldn't 'see' what you mean?

4. How do you think the blind man felt – when he saw people looking like trees? – when he saw clearly?

5. Make a list of some situations you have heard, or seen, or read about, where you feel people have 'blinded' themselves to what is right and just.

6. How can we encourage people to take their 'blindfolds' off?

7. Are we walking around 'blindfolded' ourselves? See if you can recognise any prejudices in yourselves, and pull those 'blindfolds' off NOW!

WORSHIP

Sing together *Open our eyes Lord* and let the singing fade into a time of quietness.

Reader 1   Ephesians 5:8-9.
It is true that you used to be darkness, but now, as
the Lord's people, you are light. So you must walk
as children of light, because light produces fruit of
all goodness and truth.

*Sing together a hymn or chorus. During the singing, each person
lights a candle and brings it back to her/his place, so that there is a
circle of light.*

Reader 2   Lord, help us
to remove all blindness and prejudice from our hearts.

All   God of light, enlighten our lives.

Reader 3   Lord, give us courage
to walk in your light
and live in your love.

All   God of light, enlighten our lives.

Reader 4   Lord, we ask you
for clearer vision
to see you and know you
more and more.

All   God of light, enlighten our lives.

Reader 1   The light shines in the darkness,

All   and the darkness has never put it out.

3:6

101

Making a garden

The person who made this model might be . . .

TO TALK ABOUT . . .

1　Create an animal – in exactly ten minutes!

2　God made us in his likeness; like him, we are *creative* – as you can definitely see! Now take an animal made by someone else, and in one minute, jot down anything the model suggests to you about the character and talents of its maker.

3　How do you think God felt about his creation? How do you feel when you know you have done your best and have made a good job of something?

4　This is an older creation story. How is it different from the first story we read?

5　What can we find out about God's character from reading these creation stories?

**To read together:
Genesis 1:9-13
Genesis 2:4b-9**

WORSHIP

Sing *Morning has broken*, letting the singing fade into a time of silence.

Reader 1 Genesis 1:26-31.
Then God said, 'Let us make people in our own image and in our own likeness, and let them be in charge of the fish of the sea, and the birds of the sky, and over all the living creatures that move along the ground.'

Reader 2 So God created humankind in the image of himself; in the image of God he created it, male and female he created them. God blessed them and said to them, 'Be fertile and have many children fill the earth and tame it. Be responsible for the fish of the sea, the birds of the sky and all the living creatures that move along the ground.'

Reader 1 Then God said, 'Look. I am giving you every
seedbearing plant on the surface of the earth,
and every tree with seedbearing fruit.
They will be food for you.
And to all the wild animals, all the birds of the sky
and every living creature which creeps
on the ground – to them I give all the foliage
for their food.' And so it was.

All God looked at everything he had made,
and he was well pleased with it.

Sing together a hymn or chorus.

Reader 1 Lord, you made us responsible for your world;

All make us wise and careful,
so that we look after it well. Amen.

4:1

Rainbows

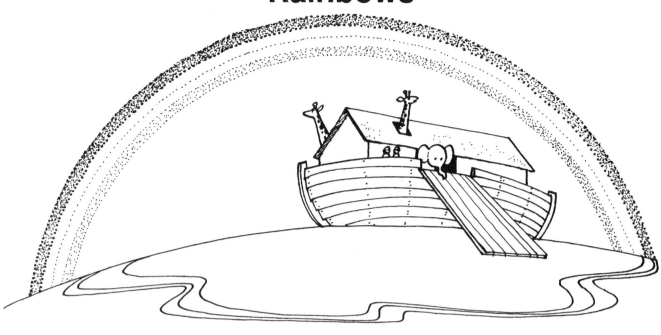

GREEN 2

Noah Quiz

1 *What were the names of Noah's sons?*

2 *Why was God going to destroy everyone?*

3 *What measurements was the boat to have?*

4 *What was Noah to take into the boat?*

5 *Why was God willing to spare Noah from destruction?*

6 *How long were they in the boat before the flood came?*

7 *How long did the flood last?*

8 *Which creature was the first to find land?*

9 *Where did the boat come to rest?*

10 *What date is given for when the ground was completely dry again?*

TO TALK ABOUT . . .

1 **What was the first thing Noah did when he touched dry land again? Why did he do this do you think?**

2 **The rainbow is the sign of a promise: what is the promise?**

3 **What qualities does God show in the story of the flood? Are there any characteristics mentioned last time reinforced by this story?**

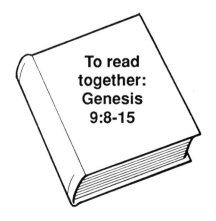

To read together: Genesis 9:8-15

WORSHIP

Sing *Do not be afraid* and let the singing fade into a time of silence.

Reader   Genesis 9:16-17.
When the rainbow appears in the clouds, I shall see it and remember the everlasting covenant between God and all the living creatures of every kind on the earth. So God told Noah, 'That is the sign of the Covenant I have established between me and all the living things on earth.'

All   The oceans lift up their voice, O Lord, they lift up their voice in a roar of pounding waves. Yet mightier than the ocean's roar, and more powerful than its pounding waves is the almighty Lord who rules over all.
(Psalm 93)

Sing together a chorus or hymn.

Reader   Father, creator, we thank you for your world;

All   help us to work with you and not against you.
Amen.

4:2

105

How many different creatures can you think of? You have one minute!

Power!

TO TALK ABOUT . . .

1 Although God has created such vast quantities and varieties, what does this reading tell us about his attitude to each particular person?

2 What does it mean to know someone really well? How many people do you know really well?

3 Do you ever feel you don't even know yourself completely?

4 If God is that concerned about each one of millions of creatures, how would he like us to treat them, do you think?

5 Make a list of five or six ways we could put this into practice in our world.

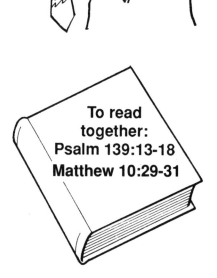

To read together:
Psalm 139:13-18
Matthew 10:29-31

WORSHIP

Sing either *If I were a butterfly* or *O Lord my God* and let the singing fade into a time of silence.

Reader 1   Psalm 36:5-9.
> Your constant love, O Lord, reaches to the heavens;
> your faithfulness to the skies.

Reader 2   Your righteousness towers like the great mountains;
> your justice is deep as the seas.

All   In your care both people and animals are safe.

Reader 1   How precious, O Lord, is your unfailing love!
> Both great and small find refuge under the shadow
> of your wings.

Reader 2   We feast on the abundant food you provide for us:
> you give us drink from your river
> of refreshment and joy.

All   For you are the fountain from which all life springs,
and in your light we can see light.

Sing together a chorus or hymn.

Reader 1   Let everything in all creation

All   praise the Lord, our God! Amen.

4:3

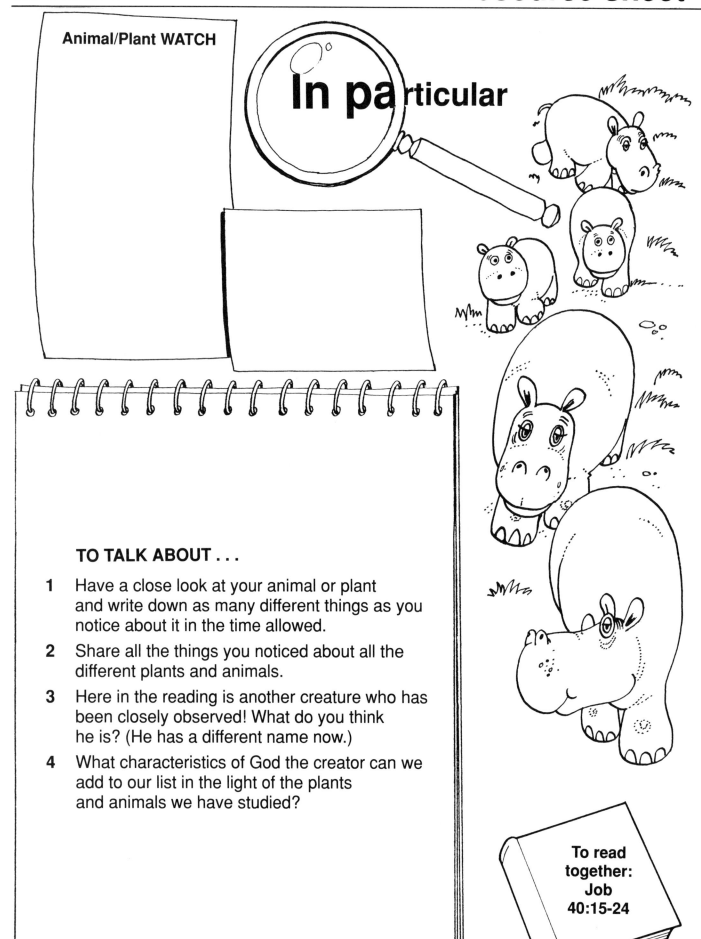

Animal/Plant WATCH

In particular

TO TALK ABOUT . . .

1 Have a close look at your animal or plant and write down as many different things as you notice about it in the time allowed.

2 Share all the things you noticed about all the different plants and animals.

3 Here in the reading is another creature who has been closely observed! What do you think he is? (He has a different name now.)

4 What characteristics of God the creator can we add to our list in the light of the plants and animals we have studied?

To read together: Job 40:15-24

WORSHIP

Sing *All the nations of the earth* and let the singing fade into a time of silence.

Reader 1   Psalm 33:4-7, 22.
   For the word of God is eternal,
   full of truth and constancy;
   he will delight in what is right and just.

All   Earth is full of his faith and love.

Reader 2   By his word the sky was created
   when he spoke the stars shone out;
   water he gathered into lakes and seas;
   with treasure he filled the ocean depth.

All   May your constant love be with us, O Lord,
   as we place our hope in you.

Sing together a chorus or hymn.

Reader 3   Praise the Lord from the earth,
   you vast sea monsters and ocean depths;
   you lightning and hail snow and clouds,
   you stormy winds that obey his command.

Reader 4   Praise him. you mountains and all you hills,
   fruit trees and cedar trees,
   wild animals and cattle,
   all you small creatures and flying birds,

All   praise the Lord! Amen.

4:4

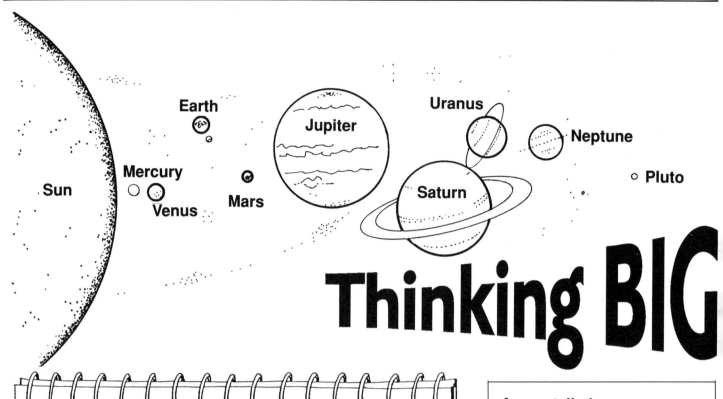

Sun Mercury Venus Earth Mars Jupiter Saturn Uranus Neptune Pluto

Thinking BIG

A constellation

TO TALK ABOUT . . .

1 Discuss what you have seen, and see if you can name all the planets in our solar system, or draw any of the star constellations.

2 Why was the psalmist surprised to find God had bothered with human beings?

3 What can we discover about God by looking at the universe he has made?

4 Do you think that we ought to accept any responsibility for the care of the universe, or should our responsibilities stay with our own planet?

5 Would it change your ideas about God and Jesus if life were discovered on another planet. If so, how?

To read together:
Psalm 8:3-9
Romans 8:38-39

WORSHIP

Sing together *Adoramus te, domine* and let the singing fade into a time of silence.

Reader 1   Psalm 29: 3-4.
> The voice of the Lord is heard in the waters;
> the God of glory thunders
> and his voice reverberates over the oceans
> in all its power and majesty.

Reader 2   Psalm 104:1-5.
> O Lord my God how great you are!
> you are clothed with splendour and majesty,
> you wrap yourself in light.
> You spread out the heavens like a tent
> and build your home above the waters,
> You make the clouds your chariot
> and ride on the wings of the wind.
> You make the winds your messengers
> and flames of fire your servants.

All   The Lord is good; his love is eternal.

Sing together a chorus or hymn.

Reader 3   The Lord is good;

All   his love is eternal. Amen.

Positively green

During the last 10 years, humans have tried to protect and improve the the environment, by:

TO TALK ABOUT . . .

1   See if you can think of five ways that humans have tried to protect and improve the environment during the last ten years.

2   Swap and share your ideas. You may be agreeably surprised at how much is done now compared with ten years ago.

3   Do you think it is possible for any good to come out of environmental disasters? Try to give examples of what has been learnt from our mistakes.

4   In some areas there is still much to be done. What is your reaction when you hear of dismal prospects for the future of our environment?

5   What conclusions would you draw from this story about Jesus?

6   What does Jesus suggest about the end of the world as we know it?

7   How might this affect the way we live in the present?

To read together:
Luke 8:22-25
Matthew
24:29-30; 36-39

WORSHIP

Sing *Jesus, remember me* and let the singing fade into a time of silence.

Reader 1 Genesis 3:17-19.
> To the man God said, 'Because you listened to your wife and ate from the tree from which I had forbidden you to eat, cursed is the soil because of you! Through painful toil you will get food from it as long as you live. It will produce brambles and thistles as you eat the plants of the land. By the sweat of your brow you will work for your food until you return to the ground just as you were taken from it.

All 'For you are dust and to dust you will return.'

Reader 2 1 Corinthians 15:20-22.
> However, Christ has in fact been raised from death, the first fruit of all those who have fallen asleep in death. For since it was through a man that death began so it is through a man that the dead are raised to life. Just as in Adam all die,

All so in Christ shall all be brought to life.

Sing together a chorus or hymn.

Reader 3 Jesus is Lord of all.

All His life sets our lives free.

4:6

Who's rich, who's poor?

a

b

c

d

e

Pic.	Rich	Poor	Why?
a			
b			
c			
d			
e			

TO TALK ABOUT . . .

1 What made you decide which pictures were of rich people and which of poor people?

2 What is poverty? How many different ways of being poor can you think of? What are they?

3 Can a poor person be rich, or a rich person poor?

4 In what way were the rich men actually poorer than the widow with her two copper coins?

**To read together:
Luke 21:1-4**

WORSHIP

Sing *Oh how good is the Lord*. Let the singing fade into a time of silence.

Reader 1 Mark 10:17-23.
As Jesus started out on a journey, someone came running up and knelt down in front of him, asking,

Reader 2 'Good teacher, what must I do to inherit life that lasts for ever?'

Reader 1 Jesus said to him, 'Why do you call me "good"? Not one person is good apart from God.
You know the commandments – do not commit adultery, do not commit murder, do not steal, do not give false testimony, do not cheat, honour your father and mother.'

Reader 2 But the man answered, 'Teacher, I have kept all these commandments since I was a child.'

Reader 1 Jesus looked him straight in the eye, and was filled with love for him. 'You only need to do one more thing,' he said. 'Go and sell whatever you possess and give it to the poor, and you will have treasure in heaven. And come; follow me.'

Reader 2 But the man's face fell at these words, and he went away in sadness, because he owned a great many possessions. Looking round at his disciples Jesus said. 'How difficult it will be for the wealthy to enter the Kingdom of God!'

Reader 3 Father, we ask you to make us rich;

All   rich in loving care, in peace and in joy.

Sing together a song or chorus.

Reader 1 Happy are you poor;

All   the Kingdom of God is yours! Amen.

5:1

Marching orders

WEEKLY BUDGET		
Expenses	**£**	**p**
TOTAL		

Situation

TO TALK ABOUT . . .

1. These were Jesus' instructions when he sent out his disciples ahead of him during his ministry on earth. Why do you think he sent them out 'poor'?

2. What might their simple, basic lifestyle help them to remember?

3. How do our materialistic lives draw us away from living as Christ's followers?

4. How did Francis find that poverty helped him to be 'rich'?

To read together: Matthew 10:7-10

WORSHIP

Sing together: *Bless the Lord, my soul,* and let the singing fade into a time of silence.

Reader 1   Psalm 127:1.
  unless the Lord builds the house,

All   the work of the builders is useless;

Reader 2   unless the Lord is protecting the city

All   the sentries stand guard in vain.

Sing together a song or chorus.

Reader 3   Psalm 23.
  The Lord is my shepherd;
  there is nothing more I need.

All   He gives me rest in green meadows of grass
  and leads me beside calm water.

Reader 3   He renews my strength.
  True to his name,
  he guides me along the paths of righteousness.

All   Even if I walk through the darkest valley,
  I shall fear no evil,

Reader 3   for you are with me;
  your shepherd's rod and staff
  give me courage and comfort.

All   You prepare a feast for me
  in view of all my enemies.

Reader 3   You honour me, anointing my head with oil;
  my cup is filled to overflowing.

All   Surely your goodness and love
  will follow me all my life.
  and I will live in the home of the Lord for ever. Amen.

Satisfying needs

A FAMILY'S NEEDS

TO TALK ABOUT . . .

1 On your card, make a list of whatever that particular animal needs in order to survive.

2 What do we need for survival and for a good quality of life?

3 Why do you think some people can survive contentedly on very little, while others are always miserable and greedy, however much they have?

4 Which of our needs as humans do you know God provides for?

5 What is the one thing Jesus wants us to be concerned about?

6 If we all did this, how would people's needs start being provided for?

To read together: Luke 12:22-31

WORSHIP

Sing *Seek ye first the kingdom of God* and let the singing fade into a time of reflective silence.

Reader 1   Luke 12:32-34.
   Do not be afraid, little flock, for it is your Father's pleasure to give you the Kingdom. Sell your possessions and give the money to charity. Make yourselves purses which will not wear out, and accumulate limitless wealth in heaven, where no thief will creep up on you and no moth destroys.

All   For wherever your treasure is,
   that's where your heart will be as well.

Reader 2   Jesus said, 'Come to me, all who are weary
   and whose load is heavy;

All   'I will give you rest.'

Sing together a hymn or chorus.

Reader 1   Lord, give us the courage to give ourselves away

All   so that we have room for your riches. Amen.

5:3

The world's poor

Needs	Action being taken

TO TALK ABOUT . . .

1   Use the newspapers and magazines to help you fill in the chart.

2   Compare charts to see everyone's ideas. The ones everybody has thought of probably show a very urgent need for help.

3   Are we Christians sometimes a bit like this? Think of two examples where we seem to say how sorry we are, but don't actually do anything about it.

4   Now think of two examples where the Church has been happy to get involved in spite of danger or disease.

5   Where do you think the Church, as the body of Christ, should be showing a more wholehearted willingness to provide for the poor, both physically and spiritually?

To read together: James 2:14-17

WORSHIP

Sing *Listen, let your heart keep seeking* and let the singing fade into a time of silence.

Reader 1   Matthew 25:31-40.
When the Son of Man shall come in his glory . . .
then all the nations will be gathered in his presence.
And he will separate them into two groups, just as
the shepherd separates the sheep from the goats.
He will place the sheep on his right hand side
and the 'goats' on his left. Then the King will say to
those on his right.

Reader 2   'Come. all of you who have been blessed by my
Father, receive as your inheritance the kingdom
which has been prepared for you ever since
the foundation of the world.
For I was hungry and you gave me something to eat,
I was thirsty and you gave me a drink,
I was a stranger and you made me welcome,
naked and you clothed me,
I was ill and you looked after me,
I was in prison and you came to visit me.'

Reader 1   Then the righteous will reply.

All   'Lord, when did we see you hungry and nourish you?
Or thirsty and gave you a drink?
When did we see you a stranger and made you welcome,
or naked and we provided clothes?
And when did we see you ill, or in prison
and we came to your help?'

Reader 1   The King will answer,

Reader 2   'In all truth I tell you, that whatever you did
for the least of these brothers of mine,
you did it for me.'

Sing together a chorus or hymn.

Reader 1   Lord Jesus, fill the world with your love

All   and let your will be done in us. Amen.

5:4

121

Spoil yourself!

Adverts which say 'SPOIL YOURSELF/TREAT YOURSELF'	Adverts which say 'Make life better for someone else' or 'Help someone you love.'

TO TALK ABOUT . . .

1. Pick out all the advertisements which encourage us to spoil ourselves or give ourselves a treat.

2. Pick out any advertisements which appeal to our wish to help someone close to us and make life better for them.

3. You can probably see from the number in each group of advertisements what the advertisers have found will make us spend most money! Share your ideas.

4. How can we make sure the sales pressure all around us doesn't push us into overdoing the care of oneself?

5. If we know that everything we have comes from God's generosity to us, what will our attitude to possessions be?

To read together:
Timothy 6:6-8
Matthew 10:8

WORSHIP

Sing together *All that I am* and let the singing fade into a time of silence.

Reader 1   Matthew 13:7, 22.
   In Jesus' story of the farmer who sowed the seed,
   some of the seed fell among thorn bushes,
   which grew up and choked the plants.

Reader 2   Jesus explained that the seeds that fell among thorn
   bushes stand for those who hear the message;
   but the worries about this life and the love for riches
   choke the message, and they don't bear fruit.

Sing together a chorus or hymn.

Reader 3   Luke 6:38.
   Give to others and gifts will be given to you – a full
   measure, pressed down, shaken together
   and overflowing will be poured into your lap.

All   For the measure you use in giving to others,
   will be the same measure God uses in giving you.

Reader 3   Loving Lord, as you have freely given to us,

All   may we give freely to others. Amen.

5:5

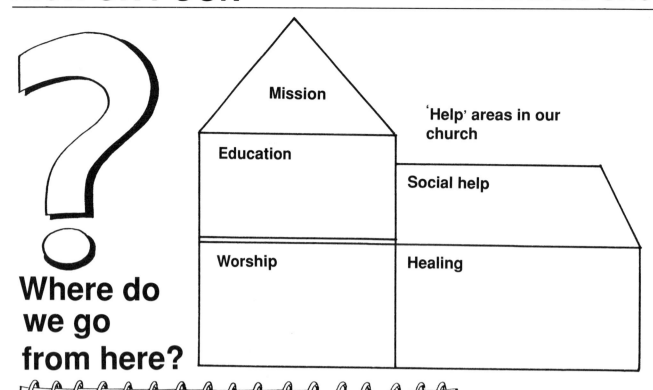

Where do we go from here?

TO TALK ABOUT . . .

1 List all the present 'help' areas, grouped as seems appropriate.

2 Are there any glaring gaps which we ought to be concerned with? If so, list these in another colour.

3 Would any area benefit from more publicity in the parish, so that more people are aware of the needs? If so, ring these in another colour.

4 God is used to starting small – he often works this way! Take one small area of your parish giving and plan to make it better.

To read together: Mark 4:30-32

WORSHIP

Sing *God forgave my sin* and let the singing fade into a time of silence. ,

Reader 1   Matthew 5:43-48.
You have heard that it was said, 'You shall love your
neighbour and hate your enemy.' But I say this to you:
love your enemies. and pray for those who persecute you,
so that you may be true children of your Father in heaven.

Reader 2   After all, he makes his sun rise on both the evil
and the good, and he sends rain on both the just
and the unjust.

Reader 1   If you only love those who love you,
what reward will you get?
Don't even the tax collectors do that?

Reader 2   And if you only ever talk to your friends,
how have you excelled yourself?
Don't even the gentiles do that much?

Both   So you must be perfect,
just as your heavenly Father is perfect.

Sing together a hymn or chorus

Reader 3   1 Corinthians 13:4-7.
Love is long-suffering and kind. Love is not jealous
or boastful or conceited. Love is never rude or self-seeking,
nor does it easily take offence or nurse grievances. Love does
not enjoy what is underhand,   but takes delight in what is
honest and true.

All   Love works in every situation; it is always ready
to trust, to hope and to persevere, whatever the difficulties.

Reader 3   Lord, increase our loving care for other people

All   and may our caring draw others to know
the richness of your forgiving love. Amen.

5:6

125

Mountains

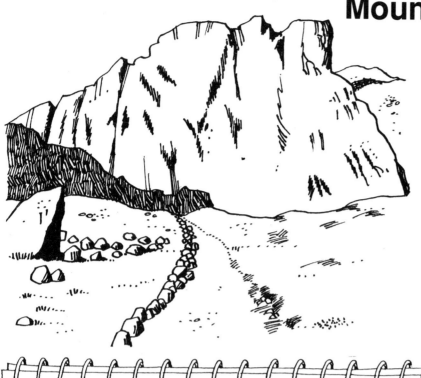

TO TALK ABOUT . . .

1   Share what you have found out about mountains.

2   Make a list of words which you could use to describe a mountain. Could some of these qualities apply to God?

3   Why do you think primitive peoples often use mountains as holy places of worship?

4   How do the psalmists use mountains as a symbol?

5   Can you think of any events of Jesus' life which took place in the mountains? If you are struggling, these references will help you: Matthew 4:1-3; Matthew 5:1; Luke 9:28-29; Luke 22:39-42; Matthew 28:16-20.

6   Why do you think the gospel writers thought it important to mention where these events took place?

**To read together:
Psalms 125: 1-2,
36:5-6,   65:6,
93:1-2**

WORSHIP

Sing together *Laudate Dominum* . Let the singing fade into a time of silence.

Reader 1 Isaiah 54:10; 55:12-13
'The mountains may be shaken
and the hills be eroded to dust,
but my love for you will never be shaken,
nor my promise of peace be eroded.'

All So says the Lord who loves you with compassion.

Reader 2 'The mountains and the hills will burst into song,
and all the trees of the fields will clap their hands.
Where there are brambles the cypress tree will grow;
myrtles will flourish in place of the nettles.'

All So says the Lord who loves you with compassion.

Sing together a song or chorus.

Reader 1 Father, we thank you

All for the way you love and care for us
every moment of every day of every year.

Reader 1 Father, we ask you

All to make us loyal in our friendships,
trustworthy in our promises,
and reliable in our responsibilities. Amen.

6:1

Commands

1 Worship no god but me

2 Don't worship idols

3 Don't use my name wrongly

4 Keep the Sabbath holy

5 Respect your father and mother

6 Do not murder

7 Do not commit adultery

8 Do not steal

9 Do not accuse anyone falsely

10 Do not envy others

Our rules for a peaceful, just society
1
2
3
4
5
6
7
8
9
10

TO TALK ABOUT . . .

1 Try making up 10 basic rules which you think would make for a peaceful, just society and write them on this sheet.

2 Swap ideas for the 10 rules.

3 Which rules were thought of most often?

4 Which rules are the most important, do you think?

5 Are these rules, for an ancient, nomadic society, in any way similar to the rules you have designed?

6 Where was Moses when the commandments were given?

7 What does the reading suggest about the relationship between God and the people?

8 Jesus summarised the commandments as 'Love God and love your neighbour'. Which commands would go in each category, do you think?

9 What were the commandments written on? What might this suggest to a nomadic people whose history was handed down by word of mouth?

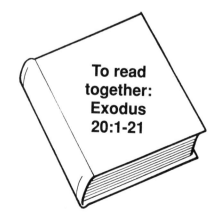

To read together: Exodus 20:1-21

WORSHIP

Sing *Love is his Word* and let the singing fade into a time of silence.

Reader 1   Jeremiah 31:33-34.
   The Lord declares, 'This is the new covenant I will
   make with the people of Israel when that time has arrived:

Reader 2   I shall plant my law within their minds and write it
   on their hearts. I shall be their God, and they shall be
   my people. It will no longer be necessary for anyone
   to teach their neighbours or their family to know the
   Lord, because everyone will know me already, from
   the least important to the most powerful. For I shall
   forgive their wickedness and never again bring their
   sin to mind,' declares the Lord.

All   Lord let your will be done in us.

Sing together a song or chorus.

Reader 1   Father, we thank you

All   for your forgiving love
   and for your constant encouragement.

Reader 1   Father, we ask you

All   to help us live according to your law of love
   wherever we go and whoever we are with. Amen.

Stone-throwing

Take 1st letter of NORMAN
Take 3rd letter of ROBERT
Take 5th letter of AMANDA

Take 3rd letter of GEORGE
Take 2nd letter of JOHN
Take 5th letter of HARRY

Our ideas for dealing with law breakers

think

TO TALK ABOUT . . .

1 Swap ideas about punishments or other ways of treating law-breakers and write them in the space provided.

2 Which of the ideas suggest punishment, which suggest deterrence, and which suggest some kind of healing or re-educating?

3 Do you think that having rules actually tempts you to behave badly, sometimes? Share your ideas.

4 In a stoning, the whole community took part. Why do you think this was?

5 'A life for a life' is certainly fair. But what are the drawbacks of such a system of punishment?

6 Which do you think more important – justice or mercy? Why?

7 Bearing in mind the society concerned in our reading, do you think stoning was a suitable punishment? Why do you think such harsh punishments were considered necessary?

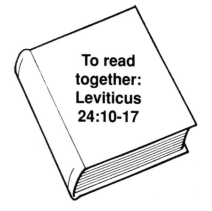

To read together: Leviticus 24:10-17

WORSHIP

Sing together *Jesus, remember me when you come into your kingdom* and let the singing fade into a time of silence.

Reader 1   Acts 7:5740.
When they heard what Stephen said,
all the members of the Council yelled out at the top
of their voice, and covered their ears with their
hands. Immediately they all rushed upon Stephen,
threw him out of the city and stoned him.
And the witnesses left their coats at the feet
of a young man called Saul.

Reader 2   And while they were stoning Stephen,
he was calling on the Lord, praying, 'Lord Jesus,
receive my spirit!' As he fell to his knees he cried out
with a loud voice, 'O Lord, do not hold this sin
against them!' And having said this, he died.

All   Father, forgive us for the cruelty and torture of our
world. Give us courage to stand firm and fight
against evil, even at the expense of our own safety.

Sing together a song or chorus.

Reader 1   Father, we thank you

All   for the work of all who struggle
against oppression and injustice.

Reader 1   Father, we ask you

All   to encourage and support
all those who are suffering pain
or imprisonment
because of their faith. Amen.

6:3

131

The temple

1 Kings 6

I think the temple looked like this

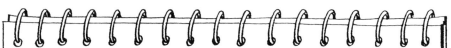

TO TALK ABOUT . . .

1   In the space above, try drawing a plan of Solomon's temple from the description in 1 Kings 6.

2   Have a look at all the plans and enjoy them.

3   What was placed in the holy of holies in the temple? (Cast your mind back a couple of sessions, or look at 1 Kings 6:19-22; 2 Chronicles 5:10.)

4   What do you think the temple was for? It may help to read 1 Kings 6:11-13.

5   Look at the number of craftsmen involved (1 Kings 5: 13-18; 2 Chronicles 2:17-18). What do you think this tells us about Solomon and the people of Israel?

6   Look at 2 Chronicles 4:1-6. What does this tell you about the worship? Can you imagine what it would have looked/sounded/smelt like?

7   If you had been one of those involved, how do you think you would have felt when the temple was finally complete?

8   Knowing the enthusiasm and care that had gone into the making of Solomon's temple, can you see why Jesus was so angry about the way the temple was being used in his day?

9   Sometimes Jesus talked of himself as being God's temple. In the light of what you now know about the temple, what do you think he meant?

To read together: John 2:13-17

WORSHIP

Sing together *Our hearts were made for you, Lord* and let the singing fade into a time of silence.

Reader 1 John 4:19-24.

   The woman says to Jesus, 'O sir, I can see that you are a prophet. Our fathers worshipped on this mountain, but you Jews say that Jerusalem is the place where people ought to worship God.'

Reader 2 Jesus says to the woman, 'Woman, believe me, that a time is coming when you will worship the Father neither on this mountain, nor in Jerusalem. You Samaritans worship what you do not know; we worship what we know, because salvation comes from the Jews. But a time is coming – and is already here – when the true worshippers will worship the Father in spirit and truth: that is the kind of worshipper the Father wants to find. God is Spirit, so people can only truly worship him in spirit and in truth.'

All Psalm 51:16-17.

All You do not take delight in sacrifices,
   or I would offer one;
   you do not want burnt offerings.
   The sacrifice you require of me
   is a humble spirit, O God;
   a broken and repentant heart you will never despise.

Sing together a hymn or chorus.

Reader 1 Father, we thank you

All for the freedom to worship you openly,

Reader 2 Father, we ask you

All to encourage and support all those for whom worship brings danger and persecution. Amen.

6:4

Strong foundations

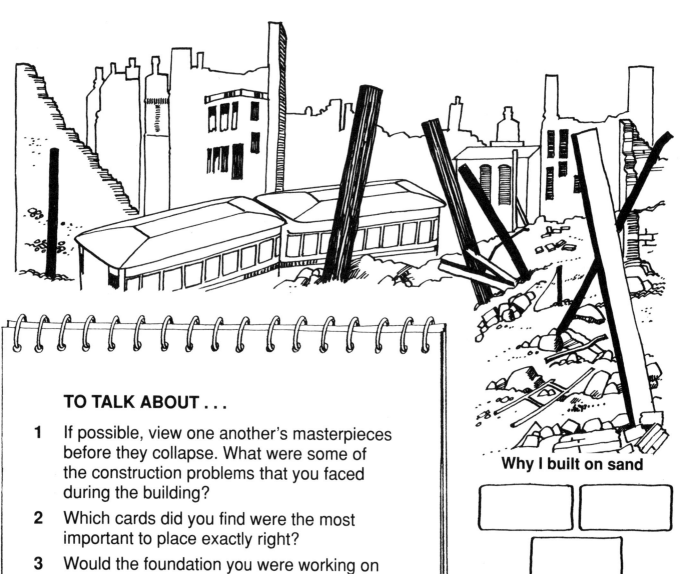

Why I built on sand

TO TALK ABOUT . . .

1. If possible, view one another's masterpieces before they collapse. What were some of the construction problems that you faced during the building?

2. Which cards did you find were the most important to place exactly right?

3. Would the foundation you were working on affect the strength of your house?

4. What would have been the advantages of building on sand?

5. When the houses were first built, would one have looked any weaker than the other?

6. Think now of your own life as a house. In what ways can we build our lives on sand or rock?

7. What might we feel are the advantages of building on 'sand'?

8. Still thinking of the story as a picture of life, what do you think the floods and storms are?

9. Can you think of any times you have witnessed a 'house' stand firm throughout 'storms' – either in your own life or in the life of someone else?

To read together: Luke 6:46-49

WORSHIP

Sing together *Build, build your Church* and let the singing fade into a time of silence.

Reader 1   Psalm 127:1.
   Unless the Lord builds the house,

All   the work of the builders is useless.

Reader 1   Unless the Lord is protecting the city,

All   the sentries stand guard in vain.

Reader 2   Jeremiah 17:7-8.
   Blessed is anyone who trusts in the Lord and relies on him.
   Such a person is like a tree growing close beside the water
   with its roots stretching out towards the stream.
   When hot weather comes it is not afraid,
   and its leaves stay green.
   In years of drought it is not worried,
   and carries on yielding fruit.

Sing together a hymn or chorus.

Reader 1   Father, we thank you,

All   for you are our strong rock and we know we can
   always trust you.

Reader 1   Father, we ask you

All   to help and strengthen all those who feel lost,
   rejected or bewildered; and strengthen our faith so
   we can serve you better. Amen.

6:5

Living stones

Living stones of our church

TO TALK ABOUT . . .

1 Fill in the stones of the drawing above with the names of all the different activities and ministries of the parish you can think of.

2 Are there any areas of need in your parish which are not being catered for? What are they?

3 Obviously stones are a strong building material. What else do we need, apart from lots of stones, to make a safe, attractive and strong building?

4 How is this like the living 'stones' of the Church?

5 In the living Church, what might be the cement that binds us together?

6 That was Paul's answer to question 4! Do you think it is true of the Church today?

7 How was the early Church different from today, and how was it very similar? You will need to look at Acts 2:42-47 to answer this question.

8 Many people outside the Church only think of it as a building. How can we make sure we really are 'a place where God lives though his Spirit'?

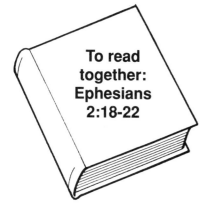

To read together: Ephesians 2:18-22

WORSHIP

Sing together *Peace perfect peace* and let the singing fade into a time of silence.

Reader 1   Acts 4:31-35.
    And when they had finished praying,
    the building where they were gathered was shaken,
    and they were all filled with the Holy Spirit,
    and proclaimed the word of God fearlessly.

Reader 2   The whole company of believers
    was united in heart and soul.
    No one claimed any possessions as their own,
    but all their resources were pooled.

Reader 1   And with great power the apostles testified
    to the resurrection of the Lord Jesus;
    rich blessings were poured out on them all.
    No one among them was ever left in need,
    because those who owned land or houses were
    selling their property, bringing the money
    from the sale and presenting it to the apostles.
    The money was distributed to everyone
    according to their needs.

Sing together a hymn or chorus.

Reader 1   Father, we thank you

All   for coming to us and filling us with joy and peace.

Reader 1   Father, we ask you

All   to fill us all to overflowing with your living Spirit,
    for you are our God, and we worship you! Amen.

6:6

137

Water! Water!

Water used today	Amount
Washing Up	
Flushing Toilet	
Washing	
Shower	
Bath	
Brushing Teeth	
Drinking & Cooking	
Other	
TOTAL	

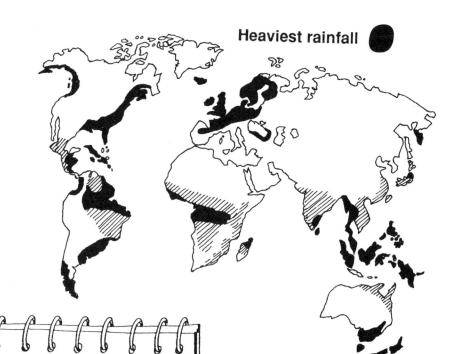

Heaviest rainfall

TO TALK ABOUT . . .

1 Was the amount different from what you expected? Which guess was nearest the truth?

2 Where does all our water come from?

3 Have a look at a world rainfall map. Where are the driest and wettest areas of our world? Do they coincide with areas of need?

4 How can we save water?

5 Many primitive people thought water was the first created substance. Pretend that you have no scientific knowledge at all. Now, from the facts you have gained from experience, why do you think they thought this?

6 In what ways are we damaging this essential ingredient of life?

To read together: Genesis 1:1-2, 6-10

WORSHIP

Sing together *Lord the light of your love is shining* (SOF4)
and let the singing fade into a time of silence.

Reader 1   Exodus 15:22-27.
Moses led the people of Israel away from the Sea
of Reeds into the desert of Shur, and they travelled
for three days without finding water. When they
reached Marah the water there was so bitter that
they could not drink it. (That is why the place is
called Marah, which means 'bitter' in Hebrew.)
So the people complained to Moses, saying,

All   'What are we to drink?'

Reader 2   Moses poured out his heart to the Lord,
and the Lord showed him a piece of wood.
When he threw it into the water, the water became
sweet enough to drink . . . So eventually they came to
Elim, where there were twelve springs and seventy palm
trees, and there by the water they pitched their camp.

Sing together a hymn or chorus.

Reader 1   As a deer longs for a stream of cool water,

All   so I long for you, O God.
I thirst for you, the living God.

Reader 2   Lord, you are the fountain of love;

All   fill us to overflowing
and bless all those who live
in the village of (name). Amen.

7:1

139

Flood

Flood stories

What happened to cars?

What happened to possessions?

What did it look like?

What happened to the crops and soil?

How deep was the water?

What were people wearing?

To read together: Genesis 6:5-22

TO TALK ABOUT . . .

1 Do you think floods are entirely destructive, or can they have some good effects? If so, what?

2 Why did God want to destroy the world which he had created out of love?

3 Have you ever felt let down by someone or something you had high hopes of?

4 Perhaps those who have could share with the others how they felt.

5 Imagine you are one of those in the ark. How do you feel as the flood waters destroy all other life?

6 Now imagine you are stepping out on to the muddy ground. How do you feel about the future?

7 How do you think God might feel about the future?

8 Do you ever think we deserve to be destroyed?

9 Has it ever occurred to you that the God who created us has the power to destroy us if he so chooses?

10 The rainbow was a sign of God's promise. What was the promise? (Genesis 9:12-17).

WORSHIP

Sing together *Rise and shine and give God the glory*
and after the singing have a time of silence.

Reader 1 Matthew 24:37-42.
As it was at the time of Noah, so it will be when the Son of
Man comes. For in the days before the flood, people were
eating and drinking, marrying and being given in marriage,
right up to the day when Noah went into the ark. And no
one understood the significance of what was happening
until the flood came and swept them all away.

Reader 2 It will be just like that when the Son of Man comes.
Then, two men will be working in the fields – one will be
taken, the other left behind. Two women will be grinding
corn at a mill – one will be taken, the other left behind.

All Be watchful, then, because you do not know
which day your Lord will come.

Sing together a hymn or chorus.

Reader 1 I depend on God alone,

All I put my hope in him.

Reader 2 Lord, protect and save us,

All for you are our strong rock
and our shelter. Amen.

7:2

141

Wells

This prophet
_____
was let down by ropes into a muddy well as a punishment for speaking God's word.
(The book after Isaiah, 38:1-13)

At this well a young girl came and gave water to a stranger's camels. She became Isaac's wife. Her name was: _____

(Genesis 24)

This man was thrown into a dry well by his brothers because they were jealous of him. His name was:

_____

(Genesis 37:12-28)

Rebecca's good qualities

_____
_____
_____
_____
_____
_____
_____

TO TALK ABOUT . . .

1   Why do you think wells are mentioned often in the Bible? (Bear in mind the climate and terrain of the Holy Land.)

2   Imagine you are collecting water for your family and notice the well is nearly dry. What worries and plans go through your mind.?

3   Why do you think the servant thought this was a good way of choosing a suitable wife for Isaac?

4   What good qualities did Rebecca show?

5   Compare her reaction with that of the Samaritan woman whom Jesus asked for a drink (John 4:7-9).

6   Jesus referred to himself as a well. Now that you know something of the importance of wells in their society, what do you think he meant?

7   Have you ever been really thirsty? If so, tell the others what it was like.

8   Have you ever felt this thirsty for meaning in life or for some particular ambition?

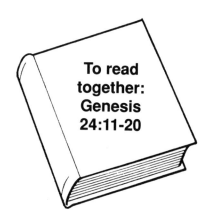

To read together: Genesis 24:11-20

WORSHIP

Sing together *Oh come to the water* and let the singing fade into a time of silence.

Reader 1   John 4:10-15.
  Jesus answered the woman, 'If you only knew
  the gift God gives, and who it is asking you
  for a drink, it would be you asking him for a drink,
  and he would give you living water.'

Reader 2   'Oh Sir,' said the woman, 'you have nothing to draw
the water up with, and the well is deep.
  So where have you got this living water from?'

Reader 1   In answer to her, Jesus replied, 'Anyone drinking
  this water will get thirsty again, but whoever drinks
  of the water I shall give him need never be thirsty
  again. But the water I shall give you will become in
  you a spring welling up for eternity.'

Reader 2   The woman said to him, 'Sir, give me this water!'

Sing together a hymn or chorus.

Reader 1   The Lord is my shepherd;

All   there is nothing more I need.

Reader 1   He gives me rest in green meadows of grass,

All   and leads me to calm pools of fresh water.

Reader 2   Father, we bring to your living water

All   all who thirst for fresh drinking water
    and all who thirst for peace, goodness and justice. Amen.

7:3

143

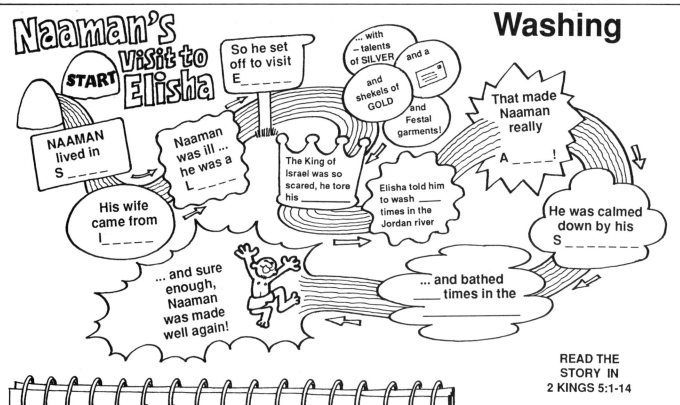

Naaman's visit to Elisha

START

NAAMAN lived in S _ _ _ _

His wife came from I _ _ _ _

Naaman was ill ... he was a L _ _ _ _

So he set off to visit E _ _ _ _ _

... with _ talents of SILVER and a

and shekels of GOLD

and Festal garments!

The King of Israel was so scared, he tore his _ _ _ _ _

Elisha told him to wash _ _ _ times in the Jordan river

That made Naaman really A _ _ _ _ _!

He was calmed down by his S _ _ _ _ _ _ _

... and sure enough, Naaman was made well again!

... and bathed _ _ _ times in the _ _ _ _ _ _

READ THE STORY IN 2 KINGS 5:1-14

TO TALK ABOUT . . .

1 If you had been Naaman, do you think you would have done what Elisha advised straight away, or after permission or not at all?

2 Why was Naaman annoyed about what he was told to do?

3 When is water used to soothe and help healing today?

4 Washing became an important ritual for the people of Israel, particularly in connection with eating, washing a traveller's feet etc. Remembering what you know of their climate and lifestyle, who do you think this ritual washing was so important to them?

5 Imagine you are one of Simon's guests. How do you feel when the woman starts washing Jesus' feet with her tears?

6 Bearing in mind what we know of the social good manners of the time, what does this episode tell us about Simon? About the woman? About Jesus?

7 Foot-washing was usually the lowest servant's job. Imagine you are one of the disciples at the Last Supper. How to you feel as Jesus bends down to wash your feet?

8 How can we 'wash one another's feet?'

To read together: Luke 7:36-39 4:4-47

WORSHIP

Sing together *River wash over me* and let the singing fade into a time of silence.

Reader 1   Psalm 51:1-2, 12.
> O God, in your kindness have mercy on me and in
> your compassion blot out my offence! Wash me
> and wash me from all of my guilt and cleanse me
> from all of my sin . . . Restore to me the joy
> that comes from your salvation.

Reader 2   Ezekiel 36:24-29.
> I shall take you out from among the nations,
> gather you up from every country, and bring you
> back to your own land. I shall sprinkle clean water
> over you and you will be cleansed; I shall wash you
> clean of all your idols and of all that has defiled you.
> I shall give you a new heart and put a new spirit in you . . .
> I shall save you from all that defiles you.

Sing together a hymn or chorus.

Reader 3   Like a dry, worn-out and waterless land,

All   my soul is thirsty for you.

Reader 3   Your constant love is better than life itself,

All   and so I will praise you.

Reader 3   My soul will feast and be satisfied,

All   and I will sing glad songs of praise to you.

Reader 4   Lord Jesus, as you washed your disciples' feet,

All   help us delight in washing
one another's feet in love. Amen.

7:4

Stormy water

Weather storms	Life storms

TO TALK ABOUT . . .

1   Galilee is notorious for violent storms that suddenly blow up and endanger boats. Can you think of a time when this happened to Jesus and his disciples?

2   Why do you think Jesus was able to sleep through the storm?

3   Imagine you are in the boat, bailing out water as fast as you can. You look across and see Jesus still asleep. How do you feel?

4   When the disciples were wondering 'what kind of man is this?', what thoughts might have gone through their minds? You might like to look at these references: Genesis 1:2; 1 Kings 19:12; Exodus 14:21; Psalm 57-1.

5   We sometimes talk of finding life 'stormy'. On the chart above, list some of the characteristics of weather storms in one column, and in the other column match them with some of the characteristics of life storms.

6   Have you ever been given peace in the middle of a bad patch in your life? If so, you may like to help the group by explaining how you felt.

Five facts about the Sea of Galilee
1
2
3
4
5

To read together: Matthew 8:23-27

WORSHIP

Sing together *Dear Lord and Father of mankind*
and let the singing fade into a time of silence.

Reader 1   Luke 8:27-35.
  As Jesus was stepping ashore he was met by a man
  from the town who was possessed by demons. For a
  long time this man had not worn any clothes, and he
  would not stay in a house, but lived out among the
  burial caves.

Reader 2   As soon as he saw Jesus he started crying out
  and threw himself down at Jesus' feet, screaming,

All   'What do you want with me, Jesus, Son of the Most
  High God? I beg you, don't torment me!'

Reader 1   And Jesus asked him,

Reader 2   'What is your name?'

All   'My name is "Many",' he answered,

Reader 1   because many demons had entered him.
  When the people from the local town and villages came to
  see what had been going on, they found the man
  from whom the demons had gone out, sitting at the
  feet of Jesus, dressed and perfectly sane.

Sing together a hymn or chorus.

Reader 3   Lord God Almighty, none is as mighty as you;

All   in all things you are faithful, O Lord.

Reader 3   You rule over the powerful sea;

All   you calm its angry waves.

Reader 4   Father, when our life feels like a raging sea

All   give us the reassurance of your peace. Amen.

Water of new life

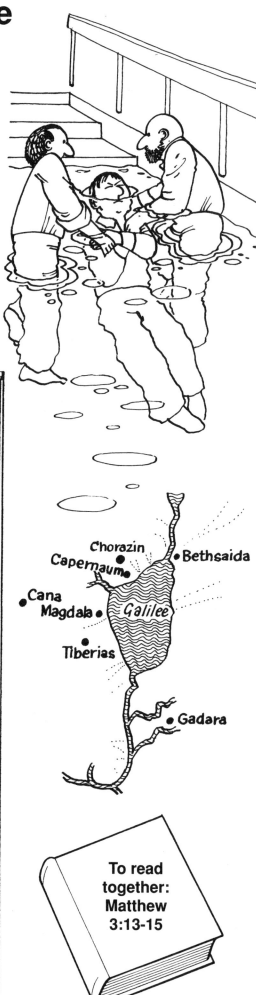

Name	John the Baptist
Mother	
Father	
Cousin	
Aunt	
Months older than Jesus	
Clothes	
Food	
Occupation	
Place of work	

TO TALK ABOUT . . .

1 If you had been one of the crowd by the river Jordan, would you have gone to be baptised?

2 What strikes you most about John's teaching – a love for people, the practical advice, the challenge, or what?

3 In the Jordan the people were completely submerged during baptism. What do you think this would symbolise? (Think back to Noah, and to the Red Sea crossing.)

4 What is symbolised by the person emerging alive from the water in baptism?

5 Why didn't John want to baptise Jesus?

6 Why do you think Jesus felt it right that he should be baptised, even though he had no need of cleansing from sin?

7 Have a look at Acts 2:37-41. The people are advised not just to be baptised, but to be baptised 'in the name of the Lord Jesus'. What is the difference?

8 What did Peter tell the people they would get if they did so?

9 Is there a danger that in making baptism freely available, we lose sight of the life-changing commitment that is being made?

To read together: Matthew 3:13-15

WORSHIP

Sing together *Veni Sancti Spiritus* and let the singing fade into a time of silence.

Reader 1   Exodus 14:21-22.
  Then Moses stretched out his hand over the sea,
  and all through that night the Lord drove the sea
  back with a strong east wind, turning the sea into
  dry land. The water was divided and the Israelites
  walked on dry ground right through the sea, with
  walls of water on either side of them.

Reader 2   Matthew 28:16-20.
  Then the eleven disciples went to the mountain in
  Galilee where Jesus had told them to go . . .
  Jesus came up to them and spoke to them.

Reader 3   'All authority in heaven and earth has been given
  to me. Go, then, make disciples of all nations,
  baptising them into the name of the Father,
  and of the Son, and of the Holy Spirit. Teach them to
  keep all the commands I have given you. And know
  this: I shall be with you always, to the very end of time.'

Sing together a hymn or chorus.

Reader 3   You welcome me as an honoured guest

All   and fill my cup to the brim.

Reader 3   I know that your goodness and
  love will be with me all my life;

All   and your house will be my home
  as long as I live. Amen.

7:6

149

Supply and demand

Type of food	Country it comes from

TO TALK ABOUT . . .

1   Which countries have provided us with this food? Use the chart above for your answers.

2   Which country provides most variety in our small survey?

3   Do you think we eat what we choose, or do the large firms really decide for us in the way they prepare and package the food?

4   Why do we eat? And how do we know when we are hungry?

5   How is God's word a kind of bread for us?

6   When would these words 'feed' you: 'Do not be afraid; I shall remain with you always'?

7   And these: 'Come to me all you who are heavily burdened and I will refresh you.'

To read together: Matthew 4:2-4

WORSHIP

Sing together *I am the bread of life* and let the singing fade into a time of quietness.

Reader 1 I Kings 19:3-6
  Elijah was terrified and fled for his life . . .
  After walking a day's journey into the desert he sat down
  under a bushy tree and wished he could die.

Reader 2 'Lord, I can't take any more,' he prayed.
  'Take my life – I'm no better than my ancestors.'

Reader 1 Then he lay down under the tree and fell asleep.
  All at once an angel touched him and said,

Reader 3 'Get up and eat!'

Reader 1 He looked around, and there by his head
  was a scone baked on hot stones, and a jar of water.
  He ate and drank and then lay down again.

All Thank you, Father,
  for strengthening us and refreshing us,
  both with food and with your loving kindness.

Sing together a song or chorus.

Reader 1 Father, we pray for all who are hungry,
  all who are starved of food, of friendship,
  of encouragement, of peace.

Silence

All Lord, feed us with the bread of life. Amen.

8:1

151

Nourishment

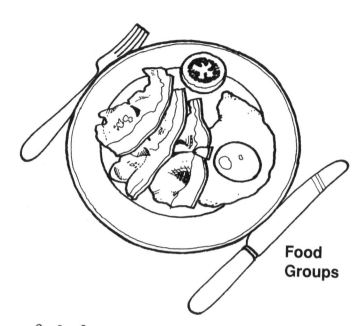

Food Groups

Cereals	Meat, Fish
Dairy Products	Fruit and Vegetables

Design a spiritual food chart

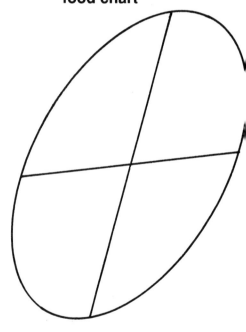

TO TALK ABOUT . . .

1 What does food do when it nourishes us?

2 Why you think 'junk food' is so called?

3 Why do you think is spiritual 'junk food'?

4 How can we get complete spiritual nourishment?

5 Have a go at designing a spiritual food chart.

6 Where would you place these references?
Genesis 1:31; Psalm 147:3; Exodus 4:12;
Matthew 18:34-35; John 20:19; Ephesians 4:1-2.

To read together: John 6:32-35

WORSHIP

Sing together *Farmer, farmer*, which is about us being made into God's bread so that the world will be fed. Let the singing fade into a time of silence.

Reader 1   Exodus 16: 2, 13-16, 31.
In the desert the whole community began complaining to Moses and Aaron that they had no food . . .
That evening, a flock of quails flew in, covering the camp; and in the morning there was a layer of dew on the ground surrounding the camp. When the dew had lifted, it left thin flakes like frost on the ground. As soon as the Israelites saw it, they said to one another,

All   'What is it?'

Reader 1   because they no idea what it could be.
Moses said to them.

Reader 2   'That is the food which God has provided for you to eat. Now these are the Lord's orders: each one of you is to gather as much of it as you need.'

Reader 1   The people called the food 'manna' (which means 'what is it?'). It was white like coriander seed – and it tasted like wafer biscuits made with honey.

All   Father, you nourish us
with food and love
and we thank you.

Sing together a chorus or song.

Reader 2   Father, we pray for all whose harvests have failed, for all who are poorly nourished both physically and spiritually;

All   Lord, we are one body, one bread;
remake us and use us
so that the world may be fed. Amen.

8:2

Feasting

A meal for . . . .

MENU

1

2

3

4

5

6

7

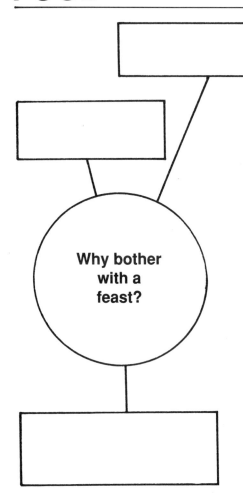

Why bother with a feast?

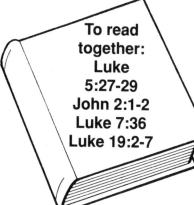

To read together:
Luke
5:27-29
John 2:1-2
Luke 7:36
Luke 19:2-7

TO TALK ABOUT . . .

1   Share the menus and vote on which is the most delicious/unusual/appropriate.

2   Why do people have feasts when a thick sandwich would probably be enough to satisfy hunger? Write your ideas in the spaces provided.

3   Why did the Pharisees object to the fact that Jesus often went to feasts? (If you are stuck on this, read Luke 7:39 and Luke 5:30.)

4   Would you think of inviting someone to your party who is despised by the rest of your group? Or who is not not wealthy enough to return the invitation? Why/why not?

5   How can we put into practice the kind of hospitality that Jesus recommended?

6   Is it ever right to feast if so many people in the world are starving?

WORSHIP

Sing together *Love is his Word* and let the singing fade into a time of silence.

Reader 1 Luke 6:32-36.
If you only love those who love you,
what thanks do you deserve?

All Even 'sinners' love those who love them!

Reader 1 And if you happen to do good to those
who do good to you, what thanks do you deserve?

All Even 'sinners' do that much!

Reader 1 And if you only lend to those you are sure will pay
you back, what thanks do you deserve?

All Even 'sinners' lend to 'sinners' if they're getting
the same amount back!

Reader 2 Instead, love your enemies and do good to them.
Lend to them without any hope of getting anything back.
And your reward will be great, and you will be children of
the Most High God, because he is kind to the ungrateful
and the wicked.

All So be merciful and compassionate,
just as your Father is merciful and compassionate.

Sing together a song or chorus.

Reader 1 Father, we pray for all those who are rich and do not
realise their need of you.

Silence

Reader 2 We pray for those who are rejected by society:
for the unwanted and the unloved.

Silence

All Father, you have been so generous to us;
help us to give freely and generously to others. Amen.

8:3

155

Fasting

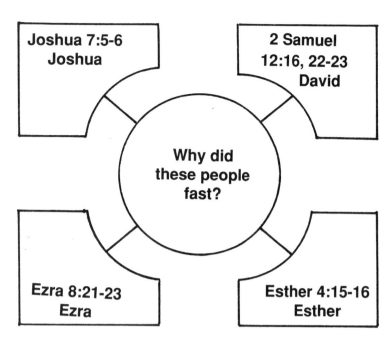

Joshua 7:5-6
Joshua

2 Samuel
12:16, 22-23
David

Why did
these people
fast?

Ezra 8:21-23
Ezra

Esther 4:15-16
Esther

Turn these stones into bread

TO TALK ABOUT . . .

1   What is fasting? Write your answers in the spaces above.

2   Why do people fast in our society?

3   What good is there in fasting?

4   When Jesus washes his disciples' feet, he is giving them an example of willing, selfless service to others. What kind of 'fasting' does this suggest?

5   Plan a fast as an act of love and an exercise in self discipline. (It need not necessarily be a fast from food. It could be sponsored.)

Our plans for a fast

To read together: John 13:12-17

WORSHIP

Sing *Here I am, Lord*. Let the singing fade into a time of silence.

Reader 1   John 13:4-9.
Jesus got up from the meal, took off his outer coat
and wrapped a towel round his waist. Then he poured
water into a basin and began to wash the disciples' feet
and wipe them dry with the towel he was wearing.
He came to Simon Peter, who said to him,

Reader 2   'Lord, are you going to wash my feet?'

Reader 3   Jesus answered him. 'At the moment you do not
understand what I am doing, but later on you will. '

Reader 2   'Never!' said Peter. 'I will never have you washing
my feet!'

Reader 3   'Unless I do wash your feet,' replied Jesus, you will
not be able to share in my life.'

Reader 2   'In that case,' said Simon Peter, 'not just my feet,
Lord, but my hands and my head as well!'

Sing together a song or chorus.

Reader 1   Father, we ask you to help us fast from all that is
unloving and unkind,

All   so that we enable others to share your banquet
of joy and peace.

Reader 2   We ask you to give us your spirit of discipline,

All   so that our lives are ruled by
your law of love. Amen.

8:4

157

Following the recipe

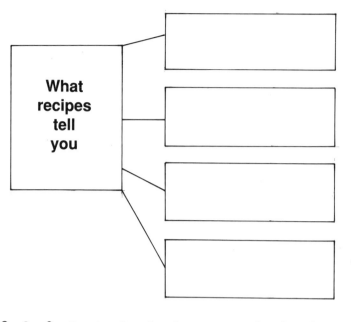

What recipes tell you

TO TALK ABOUT . . .

1   Which dishes would you be able to cook without using a recipe?

2   What kind of things do recipes tell us? Write your ideas in the spaces above.

3   What general points about cooking do we need to know to be successful (and safe) in preparing food?

4   What is the spiritual 'recipe' in the readings, do you think?

5   God's kingdom of love is what we are all helping to make. Look up these references and see how Jesus gives us practical help: Matthew 10:16; Matthew 10:19-20; Luke 11:9-10; Matthew 6:12.

6   How can we keep in touch with the power we need?

To read together: Matthew 5:14-16 John 13:34-35

WORSHIP

Sing together *Take me, Lord use my life* and let the singing fade into a time of silence.

Reader 1   Luke 9:12-17.
It was late in the afternoon when the Twelve came to Jesus and said,

All   'Send the people away, so that they can go to the local villages and towns and find some food and accommodation there, because we are in a remote area here.'

Reader 1   But Jesus said to them.

Reader 2   'Give them something to eat yourselves.'

Reader 1   They answered,

All   'We have only got five loaves and two fishes – unless you mean we should go and buy food for all these people.'

Reader 1   There were about five thousand people there. Jesus said to his disciples,

Reader 2   'Get them to sit down in groups of fifty.'

Reader 1   They did so, and everyone sat down. Then Jesus took the five loaves and the two fishes, looked up to heaven and thanked God for them. He broke them up and gave them to his disciples so they could distribute them to the crowd.

All   Everyone ate; and they all had as much as they wanted, with twelve basketfuls left over.

Sing together a song or chorus.

Reader 1   Father, we offer you ourselves for you to use;

All   take our time, our energy,
our strength, our weakness, our talents and skills.

Reader 1   Make us into the kind of people you want us to be,

All   and then use us, Lord,
for the good of your world. Amen.

8:5

159

Celebration!

Shopping list

Shopping list for _____

TO TALK ABOUT . . .

1 In the space above make a shopping list for a special celebration meal.

2 Share the lists and let the others guess what kind of celebration was being planned.

3 Why do we nearly always include food for times of celebration?

4 What are the people of Israel celebrating at the Passover?

5 What was Jesus celebrating at the Last Supper?

6 What kind of freedom was Jesus offering his followers in this new covenant?

7 What are Christians celebrating at Holy Communion?

8 Why is it so important to be well prepared for Communion?

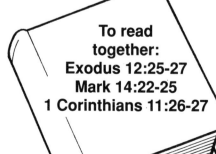

To read together:
Exodus 12:25-27
Mark 14:22-25
1 Corinthians 11:26-27

WORSHIP

The culmination of this Unit, indeed of the whole programme if it has been followed in the order given in the book, is in the celebration as a group, or within the parish, or an even larger and broader fellowship than that, of an act of Communion. Some songs and readings have been suggested, associated with the idea of 'Food', both physical and spiritual, which we have been considering. You may want to discuss other readings or songs that could be used, to emphasise your special concerns, and the work you have been doing.

PART THREE: FRANCIS!

Francis!

This lively musical play about St Francis of Assisi lasts for forty-five minutes and includes twelve songs, dancing, mime and instrumental accompaniments. Dance sequences are written in full, and there are suggestions for costumes and props. As each scene leads into the next, *Francis!* can be performed indoors or outside: a stage is not essential, and a simple production can be as effective as a more elaborate staging.

The cast of players

Crowd to be in market, inn, town, village, etc.

Woman 1	Bishop
Woman 2	Doves
Woman 3	Group of lepers including
Woman 4	an old man and a boy
Mr Bernardone	Raindrops
Mrs Bernardone	Wolf
Old man	Child 1
Francis	Child 2
Musicians	Woman
Bernard	Man
Leo	Sun
Giles	Moon and stars
Carlo	Wind and weather
Paulo	Fire
Petro	Water
2 gaolers	Earth and fruits

Scene 1

A busy market place. Everyone buying and selling. Calls of Oranges, Sweet oranges, Vegetables – best in Italy, Chickens, very cheap, ready for killing *etc.*

Two elderly women run in.

1st woman	Have you heard the news?
Crowd	What news?
1st woman	Pietro Bernardone's back from his business trip to France.
2nd woman	Ooh! Now he'll be able to see that gorgeous baby son of his. Let's tell him about it.
3rd woman	Shh! He's coming!
4th woman	Doesn't he look grand?

Enter Mr Bernardone.
Crowd gathers in quite a respectful welcome. They sing.

WELCOME, MR BERNARDONE

During the song, Mrs Bernardone comes out, carrying her baby son.

Wel-come, Mis-ter Ber - nar - do-ne.

1. We'd have held a par - ty on - ly   no-one knew which day you would be
2. Your dear wife has had her ba - by.   Yes, she's had a lit - tle son; he

back a-mong us in As - si - si, wel-come, Mis-ter Ber - nar - do - ne! Now
seems a ve - ry health-y one; we wel-come Mis-ter Ber - nar - do - ne! A

Cm   G   Cm   G   Cm

was your trip a great suc - cess? In - deed it was I must con - fess. And
boy you say, what splen-did news (it's what I'd have if I could choose). Hal-

Fm   G   Cm

was the trad - ing good in France? Just try it if you get the
-lo my dear, you look so well, or as they say in France, *très*

Cm   Fm   G   Cm   F♯dim.

chance!
belle.

wel-come, Mis - ter Ber - nar - do - ne.

G   Cm   G   Cm

167

Mr Bernardone	Now, let's have a look at this handsome young man *(takes baby)*. Welcome Master Bernardone. May you prosper in your life as I have done in mine!
Mrs Bernardone	*(takes baby back)* Aren't you going to give Daddy a smile, John?
Mr Bernardone	He's been christened John, has he?
Mrs Bernardone	Yes, that's right. It's what we agreed, isn't it?
Mr Bernardone	*(smiling)* Oh yes. But having just come back from France, I'll call my son Francis!
Crowd	FRANCIS?
Mr Bernardone	Yes – Francis!

Scene 2

During the song the crowd re-arrange set to be an inn – tables, drinking mugs etc.

GROWING UP

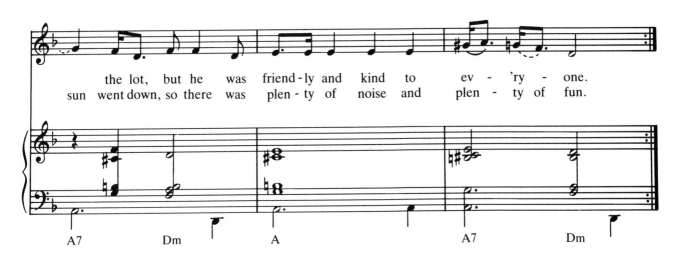

the lot, but he was friend-ly and kind to ev - 'ry - one.
sun went down, so there was plen - ty of noise and plen - ty of fun.

A7   Dm   A   A7   Dm

As the song finishes there is a burst of laughter at a joke Francis has been telling.

Old Man   Ha! Ha! That's a good one, young Francis.
Have another drink on me.

Francis   Allow me, sir, *(stands on table)* I'll treat you all to a drink.
Here – *(throws a bag of money to barman)* wine for everyone!
(wine distributed)

Crowd   Hurray! Cheers, Francis!

Enter musicians – recorder, fiddle, drum. They play.

Francis   I feel like celebrating tonight.

Bernard   You felt like celebrating last night, I remember.

Leo   *(yawning)* And the night before.

Francis   *(smiling, drags him from the seat)* And why not, Bernard?
Life's for living, don't you think? Come on, let's dance!

Musicians play rousing music.

SALTIMBANCO

Francis and friends dance in circle, clapping, with each
one in turn doing a Russian-type dance in the middle.

Everyone claps and cheers.
Messenger runs in wearily.

Francis	You look tired, Antonio. Here, have some wine. Have some food.
Paulo	Where have you come from, Antonio?
Antonio	*(gasping for breath)* From Perugia.
Francis	That's 12 miles away!
Bernard	No wonder he looks all in!
Leo	What news is there, Antonio?
Francis	Let him get his breath back first.
Antonio	I think they're planning an attack on our city.
Giles	*(angrily)* Over our dead bodies! We'll soon show them which city is strongest!
Carlo	Yes! We're ready for them!
All	That's right! We'll show them! etc.etc.
Francis	*(draws sword)* We'll be true knights, fighting to defend our liberty!
Paulo	Let's prepare ourselves. Knights of Assisi – to the rescue!

All jump up and start arming themselves.
Francis notices one, looking miserable.

Francis	What's up, Petro? You aren't still scared, are you?
Petro	Oh, no, Francis. It's just that .... well .... my father can't afford a good horse and I have no armour to speak of either.
Francis	Cheer up, Petro – that's no problem; I'll give you mine! I can always buy another suit of armour – and another horse, come to that!

Sound of battle off-stage while the women crane their necks to see,
and cheer everyone on.

Woman 3	*(screams)* Oh no – someone's been wounded!
Woman 4	Who is it? Francis or Petro?
Woman 3	It's difficult to tell – oh look, the Perugians are taking them prisoner.
Woman 4	Poor things, they look so miserable.

The women group themselves on to the front of the stage
and while gaoler changes the scene to a prison, they sing 'Some Battles You Win'.
Francis and friends are pushed up on to the stage.

SOME BATTLES YOU WIN

Some bat-tles   you win,   some bat-tles   you lose;   your wounds may   be fa-tal, or just the odd bruise;   it's al-ways   a gam-ble,   you're not free   to choose   which bat-tles   you win,   which bat-tles   you lose.

Scene 3

*As song ends the women walk off stage to the sides, and music continues
as a gaoler throws on to the stage (prison), Francis and 5 others.
Some are wounded. Petro is pushed away. He is badly wounded.
They start taking off armour and settling down.*

Francis	*(fooling about)* Welcome, sirs, to this luxurious palace! On your right you will note the fine ironwork of the ..... barred windows. Supper will shortly be served: finest quality ..... dry crusts, washed down with a good vintage of Adam's wine .... otherwise known as stale water!
Bernard	Oh, give over, Francis. Don't you ever get tired of being cheerful?
Leo	And there's absolutely nothing to be cheerful about – this prison is a dreadful hole.
Carlo	There are rats, I bet. We'll probably die here. No one would know.
Giles	Those beastly Perugians. Next time I get the chance I'll make them pay for this!
Francis	*(looking out of barred window)* Lovely view from here. Blue sky; birds, and a bit of cloud which looks ..... like your bandaged head, Petro ...... without the blood! (goes over to him) Here – have a sip of water. You look as if you could do with something stronger.
Paulo	Huh! Nothing would make that coward any better. I don't know why you bother with him, Francis. He's not worth it.
Francis	*(angry)* Paulo, an an honourable, courteous knight, you make a brilliant grape-treader! Did you take your manners off with your amour? *(softens)* Come and help me make Petro more comfortable. *(grins)* Then I'll tell you that joke I heard last week about the drunken innkeeper and his horse.
Paulo	O.K. Francis – you win! *(laughs)* I suppose you're right – we might as well make the most of it *(helps Petro)*.

*Then, grouped round Petro, they sing softly the song: 'Some Battles You Win'.
Then they settle down to sleep, and lights go out.
As lights come up the soldiers have gone and women enter, resting on brooms,
holding baskets of food and chatting together in Assisi.*

Scene 4

Woman 1	It's nowhere near as much fun in Assisi without Francis and the others, is it?
Woman 2	No, it seems dead, somehow. We haven't had a really lively party for months.
Woman 3	Do you think they'll escape from the prison in Perugia?
Woman 4	I overheard a merchant the other day saying they were going to be released.
All	Released! Set free? etc.
Woman 3	Are you sure you heard properly?
Woman 4	That's what it sounded like, anyway.

Francis and friends creep up behind women,
putting fingers to lips so that audience won't let on.

Woman 1	Well I'd give anything to see Carlo again. I think he's really handsome.

Carlo raises his eyebrows and looks pleased.
Francis teasingly pushes his shoulder.

Woman 2	Oh I prefer Francis myself – he's got a gorgeous crooked smile!

Francis pretends to look insulted, but instead
goes up to the woman 2 and covers her eyes.

Woman 2	Ahh! who on earth's that! *(touches his hands)* Oh, it can't be .... (pushes them away and turns) .... but it IS. FRANCIS! Francis, is it really you?
Francis	Of course not – I'm just a fragment of your imagination – I'm a mirage in the desert of your dreams, I'm a fleeting .....
Bernard	He's off again! Don't take any notice of him ladies .... *(they laugh).*
Woman 3	Ooh, Bernard, I hardly recognised you with that beard! I'm not sure I like it really *(she peers at it).*
Paulo	Oh, how could you – it took him months to get it like that! *(Bernard thumps Paulo)*
Woman 1	Look, I've some food here, and wine. Let's drink to your new freedom.

The women unpack the basket and pass round the bottle.

Giles	Yes, let's make the most of the time we'll be here.
Woman 4	You sound as if you won't be here for long.
Petro	We won't. We're planning to join the Crusades as soon as we've got our armour and horses organised.
All women	Oh no! What – already? etc.
Woman 2	Do you have to go to fight in the crusades as well, Francis?
Francis	Well, yes, I'm a knight, so of course I must ..... at least, I think I must.
Leo	*(finishes the bottle and hugs the ladies)* Of course he's got to come. Let's get ourselves ready – don't forget to see us off, ladies.

*They go off to collect helmets etc. while women dance, slowly
and sadly to the music of 'Saltimbanco'
played slowly in the minor key (play all the Bs as B♭).*

*As the dance finishes, Francis and friends enter,
and the women move to the sides to watch them.*

Scene 5

*The knights are busy preparing for battle again – polishing armour,
fitting on helmets etc. Francis stands with his cloth ,still, doing nothing.*

Bernard	Come on, Francis, you're dreaming again. We're due to start for the Crusades any minute. Hurry up.
Leo	*(calls)* Right – we're ready to go. Sound the trumpet.
	Trumpet sounds. All get into procession
Giles	Francis, get your helmet on – you'll be too late!
Francis	Francis *(left alone, calls)* You go. I don't think I'm meant to go with you this time. *(to audience)* If only I DID know what I was meant to do with my life.

*He turns and opens doors of an old chapel at back of stage.
They show an altar with crucifix above. He kneels down.
Music plays, and a voice (or chorus) off-stage sings 'Will You Do This For Me?'*

WILL YOU DO THIS FOR ME?

Francis   Of course! That's what I must do. But I'll need stone. And that costs money. I know! I'll sell some of father's bales of cloth. I'm sure he won't mind, if it's what I what to do. And, after all, it's in a very good cause! *Exit*

Scene 6

The crowd enters to make a market. Francis arrives selling cloth.

Woman 4   Well, Francis, I never thought you'd end up selling material!

Woman 1   This is beautiful stuff, Francis. Quite cheap, too!

Woman 2   This would make some lovely curtains for our hall!

Francis   How about these for the bedroom?

Woman 3   *(holding material up against her)* What do you think? Does it suit me?

Francis   Oh yes, madam – it brings out the colour of your eyes!

She giggles. Francis collects all the money.

Francis   There, Lord! NOW I can build your church for you! *(starts to exit)*

Enter Mr Bernardone with the Bishop.

Mr Bernardone   Where's that ungrateful son of mine? Where is he? Where is he?

Some restrain him at one side of stage. Others protect Francis at the other.
Bishop stands in the middle.
Mr Bernardone sings 'My Son, My Son'
all except Francis join in 'Francis! Oh Francis!'

My Son, My Son

My son, my son, what

have I done to de-serve a son like you? My son, my son what

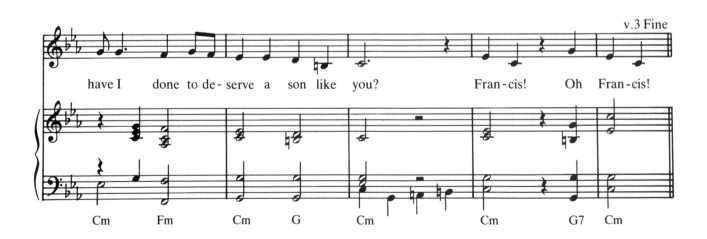

have I done to de-serve a son like you? Fran-cis! Oh Fran-cis!

Verse

1. Since the day that you were born, my son, you've had all you could de-
2. You were once my pride and joy, my son, but your brain's gone soft and
3. I'm a Chris-tian man my-self, my son, fair-ly gen-'rous with my

sire. You re-pay by bring-ing scorn, my son, and it
flab-by. Don't you think I'm jus-ti-fied, my son, if I
mo-ney, but it's got quite out of hand, my son, and I

sets my rage on fire.
seem a tri-fle crab-by? } Fran-cis! Oh Fran-cis!
find it far from fun-ny!

| Mr Bernardone | *(bows down to Bishop)* I beg you to make my son see reason. |
| Bishop | Francis, my child, it is true that you took the money for a good cause. But all the same, it really belongs to your father, and it must be given back. |

Francis   *(kneeling)* There, then, father, is the money.

He lays the money at his father's feet and sings 'I Give You Back'.

I Give You Back

son, sir, I be-long to One where I firm-ly

Am   Bm   E7   B7

pray I may re-main, and call my Fa - ther,

E   Am   Gm   Am

my hea-ven-ly Fa - ther; have I made it plain?

Fm   Am   E7   Am

During the song he takes off cloak and shirt, socks, trousers and shoes.
Bishop puts a cloak around him.
The Bishop snaps his fingers and two women bring in a brown habit,
which Francis puts on as the crowd repeat his song.
Most of the crowd disperses.

Scene 7

Francis now appears in brown habit, tied with rope belt.
A few town people watch him go as they sweep, clean the woodwork etc.

Francis
So here I am, poor. No money. No luggage. *(looks behind)* No home. *(looks up and raises arms)* Here I am then, Father. Use my life as you wish! I'll be YOUR knight and serve you as well as I can! *(pause)* And how lovely it feels to be free.

As he walks round the stage and down round the audience
the townsfolk sing 'Francis, Francis'.

FRANCIS, FRANCIS

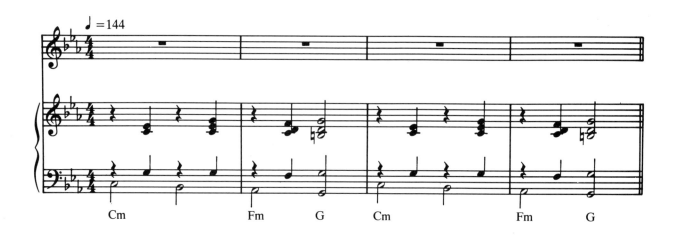

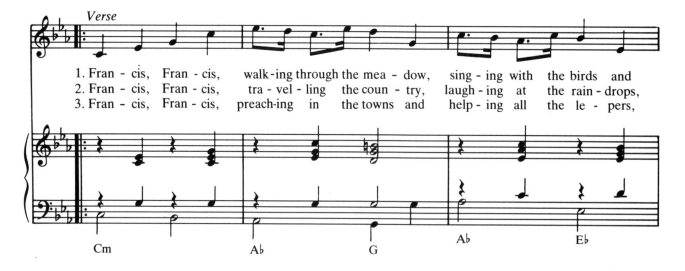

*Townsfolk go off, taking props with them.
Doves appear on stage. Francis gives them crumbs.*

Francis   Hello, my little sisters! Listen!,
                  I have something very important to tell you.

*Francis sings 'Sing His Praise', and the doves dance to the song
(see page 199 for their movements).*

Sing His Praise

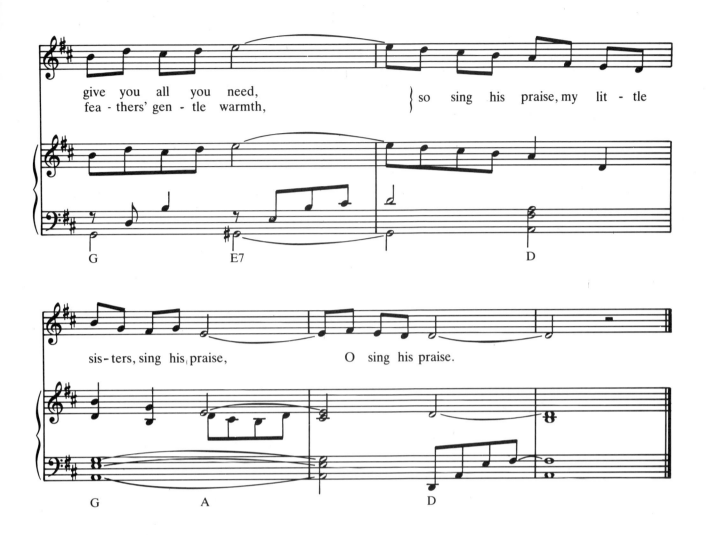

give you all you need,
fea - thers' gen - tle warmth, so sing his praise, my lit - tle

sis - ters, sing his praise, O sing his praise.

The doves gather round Francis, dance and fly off.
Francis starts building with stone blocks.
Two friends turn up, in rich cloaks.

Bernard Hallo, Francis. What are you doing these days?
It's dull without you.

Francis Hallo, Bernard. Good to see you, Leo. I'm repairing this church.
It was falling down. God asked me to rebuild it.

Leo Why ever spend your life doing that?

Francis *(smiling: they all sit)* I'll try to explain.

During the next song the two friends take off their cloaks.
Underneath they are wearing habits. All work together, singing.
See page 200 for their movements.

SIMPLY THIS

Look at the world with each one fight-ing,

fight-ing hard for what he can gain, fight-ing more

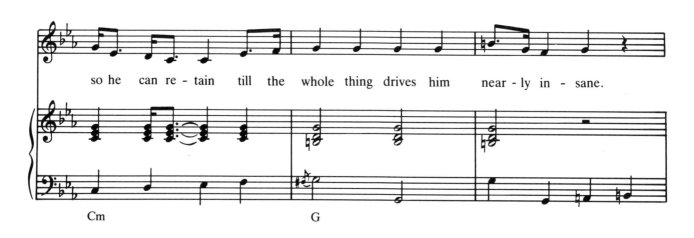

so he can re-tain till the whole thing drives him near-ly in-sane.

Francis	Well, It's time for some food, I reckon.
Leo	Good – I'm starving. Where is it?
Bernard	Yes, I can't see any food, Francis.
Francis	*(gives each an empty bowl)* Here it is! We own nothing, remember. So we beg for people's scraps.
	Bernard and Leo make faces at each other
Both	Ugh!
Francis	*(laughing)* You get used to it after a while. It helps US to be humble and it helps THEM to be generous!

Scene 8

As 'Francis, Francis' is resung,
Francis and friends wander round among the audience
asking for scraps of food.
They eventually end up on stage eating it,
and as they finish, lepers start to arrive, bells ringing.

Bernard and Leo cringe away from them.

Bernard	Francis! Keep away! Don't you realise what these people are? They're lepers!

Francis walks towards them and stretches out his hand.

Leo	Don't touch them, Francis, you fool. You'll catch the disease.
Francis	*(tending them)* Keep your hair on, Leo. These people need our help. Are you going to get me some fresh water or not? *(to leper)* how does this hand feel today, sir?
Leper	God bless you, Francis, I can't feel it at all now! But I feel happier than I've ever felt before. You're a real friend to us – the only friend I've known.
Bernard	*(walks timidly forward)* Got a spare bandage, Francis? I'll sort this young one out. *(he settles down with a small boy, bandaging his leg)* Now, little fellow, we'll make you look like a crusading knight shall we?
Boy	Is that what you are, sir?
Bernard	I used to be, son .... but now I've found a .... different way to serve.
Boy	How do you mean?
Bernard	Well, what it comes down to is simply this – *(sings 'Give yourself completely away' (See 'Simply This') then Francis and Leo grin and join in '....and God will make you rich that day'.)*

Bernard lifts boy onto his shoulders and they dance round.
'Rich in his love, joy etc.' ending in laughter. Lepers leave.

Lepers	Good bye – God bless you for your kindness – we'll see you again tomorrow.
Leo	Now it's starting to rain! I suppose we just enjoy it, do we Francis? *(looks glum)*
Francis	How did you guess, Leo! Sister Water is very good to us – we could never live without her could we?

During the singing of 'Sister Water', Raindrops appear and dance,
a few at first, and the friends sit and watch them
(for their movements, see page 202).

SISTER WATER

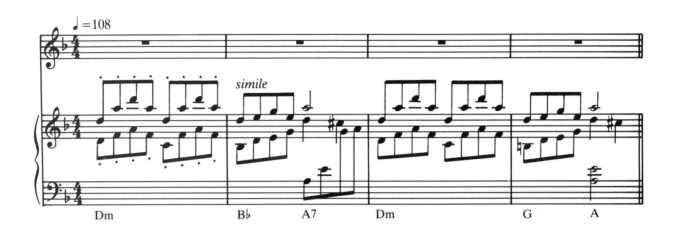

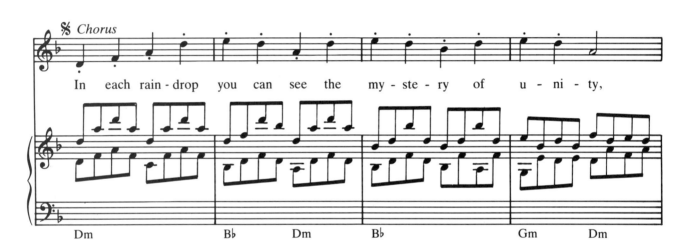

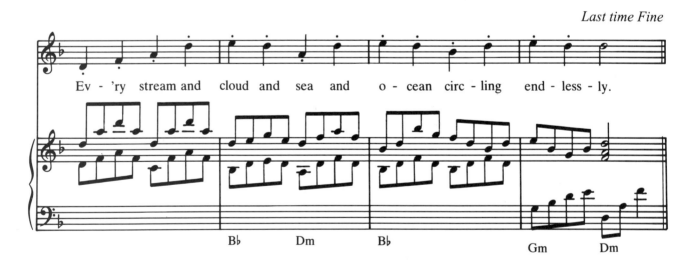

1. Sister Water, falling as rain, shows me a-gain the face of my Lord.

2. Sister Water, so pure, you can cure and soothe us all.

3. Sister Water, so humble, when we stum-ble through our pride we'll think of you.

Bernard, Leo and Francis dance with the rain.
It becomes a storm, then clears.

Scene 9

Francis   This village seems deserted.
(shouts) Where is everyone?

Villagers creep out, hesitantly and quietly begin to sing 'The Wolf'
(for their actions see page 203).

THE WOLF

We shut our-selves in

ev-'ry night, that's right! We make sure all the locks are tight, that's

right! We shi-ver and we shake with fright, that's right! Be-cause we know the

wolf may bite; he just might! 1. He comes to steal my chick-ens, he
2. This foot was bad-ly nib-bled, he

Dm   A   Dm   Dm   Gm   Dm

D.S. (to Chorus)

e-ven took my cat, he stole my lit-tle ba-by and you can't get worse than that.
in-ter-rupts our chat, he near-ly bit my hand off and you can't get worse than that.

Gm   Cm   Gm   Cm   A   Em   A7

On hills behind them the wolf listens, joining in the singing with howls.
As song ends he leaps down and all run away, screaming, except Francis.

Francis   Come nearer, brother wolf. I shan't hurt you. Sit! *(wolf sits)*
Now listen, brother wolf. I expect you are very hungry? *(wolf nods)*
And of course you have to eat! *(wolf nods)* I don't suppose the
people taste that good, do they? *(wolf shakes head)* Now you're a very
gentlemanly wolf, I can see. *(wolf nods, looking proud)* And you'd like
it if they let you share the warmth of their fire? *(wolf nods)* And gave
you juicy bones? *(wolf nods)* Then I will tell the people they must
feed you. *(wolf nods vigorously, wags tail)* And in return – you will be
a gentle wolf? As God, your father wants you to be? *(head on one
side, then resigned, agrees)* There's a good brother wolf. Shake paws.
(strokes him)

Villagers creep out.

Francis   Don't be afraid. He has promised to be gentle,
so long as you feed him.

Child 1   Here's a bone, brother wolf.

Child 2   Want one of my sweets?

Man   Have a drink of water, brother wolf.

Wolf enjoys all the fuss.
All the villagers and all players come in.

Woman   Francis, can you help us live how we're meant to?
             You seem to know God so well – you see him everywhere.

Man   Yes – please help us understand.

Francis   It is really very simple – God made everything in this world
             including us, and he loves us very much. Have you ever noticed
             what a beautiful world it is?

The finale to the performance is commenced as Francis leads the cast in singing
the 'Canticle Of The Sun'. For performance notes see page 203.

CANTICLE OF THE SUN

1. Bro-ther Sun,   who gives the
2. Sis-ter Moon,   and all the
3. Bro-ther Wind,   the cloud and
4. Bro-ther Fire,   who light-ens
5. Sis-ter Wa-ter,   who is so
6. Sis-ter Earth,   our mo-ther

day,   and light-ens us with bright-ness here,
stars   in   hea-ven's dis-tance bright and clear,
air,   all wea-ther   ei-ther rough or fair
night, who flames with beau-ty and with joy,
pure,   so   use-ful   to us in our lives,
dear,   sus-tain-ing   all and rul-ing all,

Chorus

and shows the beau - ty and the ra - diance of God's love.
who show how pre - cious is the ma - jes - ty of God.
by which is gi - ven to so ma - ny crea - tures life.

his power - ful strength re - flects the power - ful - ness of God.
and gent - ly teach - es us to love hu - mi - li - ty.
pro - duc - ing ma - ny fruits, with co - loured flowers and herbs.

Let

him
her } praise you, dear Lord, to you a - lone ho-nour and praise are due, and we will
them

wor-ship you in all the world that you have made. made.

vv.1–5 D.C. v.6

The Songs

WELCOME MR BERNARDONE
This should be rousing and cheerful. During the song Mr Bernardone walks majestically up the centre on to the stage and the crowd respectfully bow and curtsey. Solo voices are used where appropriate.

GROWING UP
This needs a 'Blues' feel about it, particularly in the instrumental parts between the verses. The scene change should take place slowly and leisurely, in keeping with the song's rhythm.

SOME BATTLES YOU WIN
This can be sung first in unison, then in parts.

WILL YOU DO THIS FOR ME?
You may like to record this beforehand, using echo-effects. Otherwise a solo voice sings over a hummed accompaniment. Then the song is repeated with a full, rich sound as Francis slowly gets up and walks to the front stage.

MY SON, MY SON
This should sound full of anger and fury, and is a solo for Mr Bernardone. The townspeople join in the repeat of the chorus each time and 'Francis O Francis'. During the outburst, they mime their agreement, disagreement, sympathy and rejection.

I GIVE YOU BACK
The sadness and poignancy of the first part of this song turn into a more confident decision in the second part. It is sung first as a solo by Francis and then repeated by onlookers as Francis is dressed in his new clothes.

FRANCIS, FRANCIS
This is lively and cheerful. Between the verses the music is sung to 'la' the first time and whistled the next two.

SING HIS PRAISE
This can be sung first as a solo by Francis and then by the full choir as the doves dance.

Little sisters, gather round and I will tell you how	*Doves 'fly' round one behind the other in a circle;*
your father loves you; now	*stand still and hold hands facing inwards;*
and ev'ry moment that you live,	*run into centre, stretching linked hands upwards;*
he loves to give	*run back;*
you all you need,	*drop hands and turn outwards, arms stretched for flight;*
so sing his praise, my little sisters, sing his praise,	*fly about all over the stage;*
O sing his praise.	*come to settle round Francis, eating 'crumbs' from his hand, perching at his feet etc.*
Little sisters gather round and I will show you where	*Francis stands up and doves flutter round him;*
to see his face: it's there	*they stop at centre stage, Francis kneels on one knee, his arm round two doves;*

wherever freedom flies	*he raises his arms and all doves fly free.*
and kindness lies	*Doves flutter back,*
like feathers' gentle warmth,	*and preen their feathers;*
so sing his praise, my little sisters,	*all whirl round, including Francis;*
sing his praise,	*they gather to join hands in a line across the stage, Francis centre, and*
O sing his praise.	*run forward swinging arms up. Doves 'fly' around free and off stage, waving to Francis as they go.*

Simply This

First time Look at the world with	*Bernard and Leo sit, one each side of stage. Francis takes 3 steps from the back;*
each one fighting,	*appeals to Bernard and Leo;*
fighting hard for what he can gain,	*grabs Bernard and grapples with him; Bernard drops to the ground.*
fighting more so he can retain	*grabs Leo and grapples with him – Leo falls to the ground,*
till the whole thing drives him nearly insane.	*clutches head and walks round in small circle (8 steps);*
Misery,	*turns to Bernard, kneels on one knee cupping chin in hands;*
anxiety,	*turns to Leo, pulling hair out or shaking. Bernard and Leo stand up;*
depression and obsession	*they approach menacingly,*
till we're	*arms forward, fingers spread,*
locked up in a prison	*till Francis is 'imprisoned'.*
and we've thrown away the key:	*Francis pretends to throw key out forwards.*
that way we'll never be free.	*Francis grasps the 'prison' wrists and peeps under them, crouching.*
But turn to Christ,	*Francis slowly stands up,*
hand him your life,	*extends both hands out, palms up, over prison bars.*
and you walk like a freed man into the light;	*Francis takes four strong strides forward, pushing away each bar arm in turn. Bernard and Leo, once their prison is broken, stagger back then sit on the floor, watching. They look sceptical.*

and the world becomes alive with his grace.	*Francis runs and pulls Bernard to his feet;*
You notice his love all over the place	*they walk across to Leo and Francis pulls him to his feet;*
and you're free to live	*walking between Bernard and Leo with arms on their shoulders, Francis leads them round and back to the centre:*
and you're free to give,	*they split and whirl round with a leap, arms high.*
and what it comes down to is simply this:	*Francis kneels on one knee others lie on floor with chins cupped in hands watching him.*
give yourself completely away	*Francis points with both hands to himself, then flings arms outwards.*
and God will make you rich that day;	*Francis stands up, runs forward and does head over heels, or a high leap or anything else acrobatic. Bernard and Leo roll over and over to front of stage.*
(music for one bar)	*All jump up and form 'conga' one behind the other.*
rich in his love; rich in his joy;	*They dance round doing the 'conga' ending back stage.*
rich in his	*They split and walk slowly forwards together, arms down, palms forward*
peace.	*Francis stands centre, 'at ease' with arms high; Bernard and Leo kneel either side on one knee, both arms up towards Francis.*

Second time

	All three run to the back and walk forward three steps as the song begins. The actions are the same as before until:
But turn to Christ, hand him you life,	*Bernard and Leo unfasten their cloaks;*
and you walk like a freed man	*Bernard and Leo fling their cloaks away. Underneath they are wearing brown habits.*
into the light;	*they hold arms with Francis as all three take strong strides forward;*
and the world becomes alive with his grace.	*each walks in small circles miming their wonder (Francis looks up at the sky, Bernard bends and 'picks' a flower, Leo follows the flight of a bird with his finger);*

You notice his love all over the place	*they join hands and do a knees up, or skip round in a circle;*
and you're free to live	*all do backward roll;*
and you're free to give,	*all do forward roll;*
and what it comes down to	*all kneel on one knee;*
is simply this:	*hands on thighs;*
give yourself	*point with both hands to themselves;*
completely away	*then fling arms outwards, smiling at each other.*
and God will make you rich that day;	*Bernard and Leo make a hand seat, Francis jumps on and they run forward.*
(music for one bar)	*Francis jumps down and they form 'conga';*
rich in his love	*they do the conga,*
rich in his joy	*finishing at the back;*
rich in his	*they walk slowly forward, Francis with arms round their shoulders.*
peace.	*Finish as before.*

SISTER WATER
Accompany this with triangles, glockenspiels
and xylophones etc. During the 'plainsong'
verses have a 'shimmer' of shakers or
tiny bells.

Use very small children for the Raindrops'
dance. During the chorus they jump (as
lightly as possible!) on the beat all over the
stage. i.e. In eách ráin dróp yóu cán sée, etc.

Verse 1

Sister Water, falling as rain,	*They run to make a line from the centre front to centre back, one behind the other, so that they are all hidden behind the front raindrop who holds a large cardboard 'cloud'.*
shows me again the face of my Lord.	*Heads pop out of both sides of the cloud and then all the children run out to a space on the stage.*

Verse 2

Sister Water, so pure,	*They run to make a large circle.*

you can cure and soothe us all.

Slowly they raise their arms forwards up, upwards, and turn round.

Verse 3

Sister Water, so humble,

They run to make a semi-circle line across the stage facing forwards.

when we stumble through our pride we'll think of you.

At 'stumble' they all fall down.

For the storm, the chorus is repeated twice only faster, and the jumping is heavier. Francis, Bernard and Leo jump as well. A thunder board and flashing lights add to the effect. Then the melody is played on glockenspiel or bells without singing, and the raindrops jump quietly off, two of them first pulling down a painted rainbow backstage.

THE WOLF
The chorus should begin like a distinct whisper which gradually gets louder as the villagers creep further out. Individual voices sing each line (two or three for 'he interrupts our chat') and bandages show evidence of the wolf's activities. At the end of each verse the wolf howls and the villagers rush out of sight creeping up again during the chorus.

CANTICLE OF THE SUN
This song should build up in layers through each verse to a rich, majestic final chorus. As each verse is sung, a banner is carried, with dancing attendants, up through the audience to the stage.

Verse 1 Brother Sun	Treble recorders and violins.
Verse 2 Sister Moon	Triangles and glockenspiels.
Verse 3 Brother Wind	Shakers and flute (or descant recorders).
Verse 4 Brother Fire	Cymbals and clappers.
Verse 5 Sister Water	Bells and pizzicato violins.
Verse 6 Sister Earth	Drums and descant voices.

Costumes and Props

Francis was born in Italy in 1181 or 1182, so twelfth and thirteenth century European dress is what to aim for: basically, long dresses for the women, tunics and tights for the men, and rich cloaks for the wealthy. The Franciscan habits were made from rough hessian and tied with a length of rope. Bare feet, or sandals may be worn. Crusaders wear a white tunic (cut from old sheets) with a red cross painted on it.

Swords can be made from short canes covered in foil, with a cross piece lashed to it and wound with coloured wool.

Helmets can be made from a cardboard 'cap' stapled together. A length of material is stapled around the bottom and the whole thing sprayed with silver paint.

More sheeting can be used for *doves' costumes.* Cut out the basic shape, sew (a) and (b) together to make a hood, and tie the tapes on to the wrists and arms of the doves. White socks, shorts and T-shirt are worn with the wings.

Raindrops might wear blue or white, with milk-bottle top belts, necklets, bracelets and anklets. A piece of tinsel can be tied round the head.

The wolf can be dressed all in grey, with grey socks on his hands and a grey balaclava on his head. Short ears can be tacked on to this.

The *banners* for 'Canticle Of The Sun' can be made as collages in either paper or material. Garden canes make convenient supports.